Greetings from

TOMMYWOOD

From Award-Winning Journalist and Producer

TOM TEICHOLZ

The First Installment of the ***TOMMYWOOD*** Series,
a Collection of Columns and Writing on Arts and Culture

A PONDWOOD PRESS BOOK

PONDWOOD PRESS
1424 4th Street, Suite 229
Santa Monica, CA 90401

FIRST TRADE PAPERBACK EDITION

The majority of the articles in this collection first appeared in print in *The Jewish Journal of Los Angeles*, some in slightly different form and can also be found at tommywood.com.

Set in Minion
Printed in the United States

10 9 8 7 6 5 4 3 2 1

ISBN 978-0-9883964-4-9

Publisher's Cataloging-in-Publication data is available upon request.

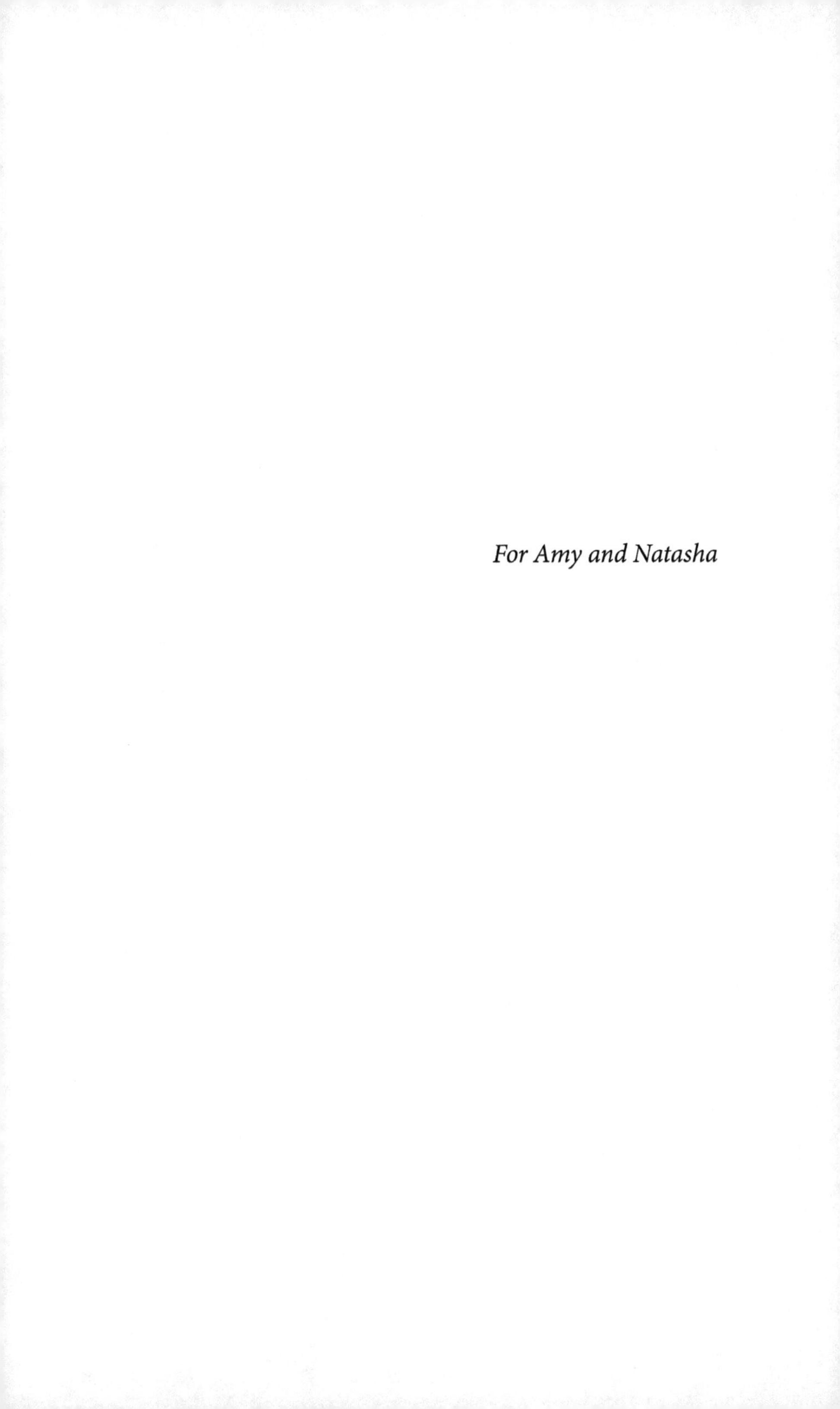

For Amy and Natasha

Contents

Also By Tom Teicholz

Wilshire Boulevard Temple and the Warner Murals: Celebrating 150 Years
by Tom Teicholz, Oro Editions, San Francisco, CA 2014

The Trial of Ivan The Terrible: State of Israel vs. John Demjanjuk
by Tom Teicholz, St.Martin's Press, New York, New York, 1990

Like No Other Store: Bloomingdale's and the Revolution in American Marketing by Marvin Traub and Tom Teicholz, Times Books / Random House, New York, New York, 1993

Conversations with Jerzy Kosinski
edited and with an introduction by Tom Teicholz, University Press of Mississippi, Jackson, Mississippi

Conversations with S. J. Perelman,
edited and with an introduction by Tom Teicholz, University Press of Mississippi, Jackson, Mississippi

The Jewish Role in American Life, Casden Insitute Annual Study, Volume 1,
by Barry Glassner, Hillary Lachner, and Tom Teicholz, USC / Casden Institute, Los Angeles, CA.

Greetings from Tommywood (Volume One)
by Tom Teicholz. 2014

Son of Tommywood (Volume Two)
by Tom Teicholz 2014

Tommywood III: The Column Strikes Back
by Tom Teicholz 2014

Tommywood Jr., Jr.: The Gospel According to Tommywood (Volume Four)
by Tom Teicholz 2014

Fast Furious Tommywood (Volume Five)
by Tom Teicholz 2014

Close Encounters of the Tommywood Kind (Volume Six)
by Tom Teicholz 2014

Other books and anthologies containing Tom Teicholz's work:

Conversations with Isaac Bashevis Singer, University Press of Mississippi, Jackson, Mississippi

Writers at Work, Volume 8, The Paris Review Interviews, Viking/Penguin, New York

Encyclopedia Judaica, Second Edition. Tom Teicholz, American Film and TV editor

Introduction

Los Angeles is as much concept as city, set in a desert that flows to the sea; that ends in the sand where an ocean begins whose horizon recedes in the sunset; a city where émigrés and the children of immigrants have come to make their dreams come true. It is a mix of the sublime and the obvious, of the new and the nouveau, of the selfless and the selfish. It is as delicate as the quality of the light, the air and the surf; and as ephemeral. It is about the outdoors and about what happens behind closed doors. Life is lived in LA in a garden of unlimited potential, a crap game where people believe that, at any moment, one well placed bet can change your life. *Tommywood* covers this waterfront, filtering the landscape through a very personal lens.

Writing *Tommywood* has allowed me to explore the city I live in and become more engaged and involved in the intellectual and dream life here. I've been able to interview icons as disparate as architect Frank Gehry, French philosopher Bernard Henri-Levy and legendary producer Robert Evans. I've had a backstage tour of Disney Hall, visited a charter school in South Central, and was a given a tour of his home by painter R. B. Kitaj before his untimely death.

Tommywood has indulged my own obsessions about Bob Dylan, Randy Newman, Rod Serling, S. J. Perelman, and about Hungarians in Hollywood—about fads, trends, and games new and old, such as mah-jong. I've been able to write about the books that inspired me and to lobby for my dream of LA becoming to the start of the 21st Century as Budapest was to the beginning of the 20th: the city whose citizens are most engaged in the arts and whose very culture fosters and supports the arts. Name dropping is rampant in *Tommywood* but occasionally the names are ones we don't hear enough about in passing conversation, such as The Rambam, Tsvetan Todorov, and Isaac Babel.

I've also had the chance to profile the kind of unique personalities who make their home in LA, such as Gary Mann who runs the Traffic School of America, Jim Beloff who stages the Uketopia Ukelele festival, and singer-songwriter Jill Sobule's guest appearance on *The West Wing*. LA is all about the mix: *Tommywood*, and the people profiled in it, is my attempt to represent that.

My wife and I have a running joke where she asks me what my next column is about and I reply, "It's about me." In some way, it always is. Over the course of the years covered in this volume some columns are more personal than others, such as when I wrote about cleaning out my mother's apartment after she died. My readers tell me that those are the columns that are most universal.

So how did I get the column? Timing, timing, timing.

After being a journalist and book author in New York, I spent a decade in LA as a movie development executive. Calling friends in New York could loosely be seen as part of the job. One afternoon I was on the phone with my friend Nessa

Rapoport, telling her about my various movie projects and the progress I was making with them, or the lack thereof.

"You sound," She said politely but firmly, "like you're floating."

I was feeling a bit unmoored, it's true.

"Here's what I want you to do," she said. "Hang up the phone and call whoever is the editor of the Jewish newspaper in Los Angeles. He's going to give you a column."

"What do you mean," I said, "he's going to give you a column?"

"I know you, and I know your credits," Nessa said, "and he's going to give you a column."

There was about thirty seconds when I vacillated between following her directive or lying down and taking a nap. But Nessa had said this with such confidence that I thought "Why not?" Although I didn't know Rob Eshman, the editor of the Jewish Journal of Los Angeles, I knew several people who did.

I dialed the number of Dan Adler, a former CAA agent who had recently left the agency to work for a new business venture —he was a friend of Rob's.

"Could you call Rob Eshman and see whether he might meet with me, to see if I might do an article or write something for him?" I said meekly. Dan promised he would.

That was on Monday. I met with Rob on a Thursday and by Friday I had a column. Nothing has ever come easier. Thank you Nessa. Next time could you include a list of lottery numbers?

I like to say that my column which appears every two weeks (or so) is not a column that goes "and he or she's Jewish" but a column in which if I'm interested in it, it's Jewish. That being said, it hasn't been too difficult to find the Jewish element in any story I've written.

New York, where I came of age, is popularly regarded as the most Jewish city in the world, but in my day the Establishment culture was WASP. Los Angeles feels like the opposite—a city where Semite and anti-Semite alike share the false belief that everyone is Jewish and every institution is Jewish. I wouldn't say they are right, but to some extent, they are not wrong.

In LA, I have found myself at my daughter's after-school Jewish religious class surprised to see a notable Catholic politician picking up his grandchild. I have seen the son of one of Ronald Reagan's inner circle on the bimah with his wife, wearing a kippah, saying Hebrew prayers. When watching the Oscars I was told that the Nigerian actress nominated for her role in *Hotel Rwanda* has a Jewish mother. Yes, sometimes in LA it seems everyone is Jewish—or only one degree of separation from Member of the Tribe affiliation.

This is also true on the cultural front. Fifty years ago, LA had few institutions seriously devoted to modern art. Today Los Angeles has half a dozen world class collections or museums, such as the Norton Simon, LACMA, MOCA, the Hammer, and the Getty each founded by individuals mostly Jewish, and if they were not (as in the case of the Getty), the institutions were expanded and developed into their current incarnation by their Jewish leaders. This is in marked contrast to other cities where until recently Jews were restricted to one or two seats on the board of the main city art museum. That, too, is the story of LA, a tale of self-made and self-invented entrepreneurs, go-it-alone do-it-my-own-way types, with egos to match who created institutions in their own image.

However, in other ways this notion of LA as a Jewish city is misleading. The Movie industry which was started by Jewish immigrants are all now international corporate behemoths responsive to shareholders—and the majority of the owners are no longer Jewish. Although it is true that many Jewish executives work in the entertainment industry, as I remarked somewhere else, even though the pyramids were built by Jews no one thinks of them as Jewish.

LA is the greatest Jewish city in the world. It is also the greatest Hispanic city in the world; and the greatest African-American city in the world. That is what makes LA great.

LA is all about contradictions—that shouldn't surprise anyone: mirages appear in every desert. When I first visited Los Angeles in the early 1970s, as a teenager, what passed for culture was going to Venice to see Arnold Schwarznegger work out. Now he's our former governor and people head indoors for art, theater, film, dance, and music.

Finally, I believe in the power of culture, in the power of good books, good conversation, and interesting people to improve the quality of our lives. Writing this column has made my life so much richer. I hope reading it does the same for you.

Welcome to *Tommywood.*

Overnight Sensation

Jill Sobule on The West Wing

The Beatles on *Ed Sullivan*. Michael Jackson's Moonwalk on the *Motown 25th Anniversary Special*. Ricky Martin at the Grammys. Each of these TV appearances launched a musical career into the stratosphere. On Wednesday February 12, 2003, Jill Sobule appeared on *The West Wing*. Will lightning strike again?

If you watched the episode, you may have seen Sobule, the singer-songwriter best known for her hit "I Kissed a Girl," playing two songs in a bar as Toby and C. J. argued a moral point. For *The West Wing* it's another episode. For Sobule, it was an opportunity waiting to explode into a possibility.

Sobule has been performing for more than two decades, since she was a teenager. She has opened for Don Henley (playing in front of crowds of 20,000) and Warren Zevon, and performed at Neil Young's "Bridge" concert. She's played backup for Lloyd Cole. She's had a band and performed solo, and toured the country with her traveling guitar. Over the years, she has released five CDs, on several labels. She plays more than 100 concerts a year.

She has a career. She has a devoted following. But she wants a life. She has been able to support herself, but as she sings in one of her new songs, she "still lives like a freshman." Sobule currently has no record deal. She is working on a one-woman show. It's not so much that Sobule wants to reinvent herself, as she wants to find the audience that will allow her to live as an adult.

Part of the problem is that record companies or radio stations are no longer set up to find or reach Sobule's audience. Over the last few years, adult album-oriented radio has failed repeatedly in Los Angeles (Does anyone remember 101.9? KSCA?). Many prominent singer-songwriters, such as Randy Newman and Sam Phillips, have migrated to smaller boutique labels, such as Nonesuch records, in hope that their music will not be lost in the shuffle. There was a hope that the Internet would become a means of distribution so that smaller artists could make a better living. So far, that dream has not come true. Instead, file-sharing has weakened the major music labels without empowering or remunerating smaller labels and artists.

Sobule's songs are funny, sweet, ironic, wistful and, at times, cruel and vengeful. But she is always optimistic. She is the SpongeBob SquarePants of singer-songwriters. But where is her audience? Not buying CDs, not listening to radio. MTV hardly plays music videos anymore and they hardly play videos by artists over thirty. What's a performer to do? One thought is that Sobule's audience may be the same people who enjoy *Curb Your Enthusiasm* or *The West Wing*, for that matter. That's why Sobule's appearance holds such promise.

Sobule is a friend, and I'm a fan. I first saw her perform about eight years ago at Genghis Cohen. I usually see her when she's in town. And yes, we have collaborated: the summer before last we pitched a sitcom together with playwright-screenwriter Seth Greenland. The show's premise was "how do you stay true to your art when everyone around you is telling you to be an adult about your chosen career?"

I'm shocked, shocked, shocked that it didn't sell—actually, I am.

More recently, in December, Sobule performed at an ACLU benefit honoring Samuel Paz, Barry Levinson, Fred Goldring, and Ken Hertz (her attorney). Goldring and Hertz's award was presented by *West Wing* creator Aaron Sorkin. Before the evening was over, Sorkin had decided to write Sobule into an episode.

Which is why, late on a Wednesday night in early February, I found myself at the Pig and Whistle bar in Hollywood. For most of the day the bar had been taken over by *The West Wing*. Leslie Linka Glatter was directing and the bar was full of actors and legions of production people; equipment cluttered the room. Sorkin had been by earlier; Lewellyn Wells was there now. It'd been a long day and there were still more takes to be done.

Sobule was enjoying herself, playing cover songs between takes, with the cast and crew singing along—you've not lived until you've heard Brad Whitford's "Sunrise, Sunset."

"I could get used to this," she said.

If you ask Sobule if she's ever acted before, she answers: "I was Queen Esther in the Purim play." Her family has great intellectual and performance art creed: her great uncle worked on the Manhattan project; one of her cousins is Sarah Boxer, the *New York Times* contributor; another is the professional wrestler Goldberg.

Sobule grew up in Denver, Colorado, and attended St. Mary's academy—don't ask. One of the first original songs she performed at school, "Jesus Played the Dreidel," got her into trouble. At nineteen, she was discovered performing on the streets in Spain. The rest, as they say, is one gig after another.

There are moments in our life when our fate seems decided. At an early age, parents ask us what we want to be when we grow up. At some point we start coming up with answers. We are typecast or cast ourselves in such roles as doctor, lawyer, teacher, artist, businessman, among many others, or we drift until we find ourselves doing what it is we do. What happens if that notion of ourselves or that notion of how the world works is more appropriate to a teenager than an adult? What if we get to do what we love, but we want to buy a home, raise kids, settle down? All these thoughts swirled though my head as I watched Sobule doing take after take through the long night.

Sobule will always write and perform. But there are so many artists who, mid-career, still struggle. Los Angeles is filled with people waiting for their close-up. Every success, they say, was a failure until the night before. You're standing at the roulette table and you don't want to leave.

On February 12, NBC aired *The West Wing* episode, "Inauguration Day: Over There." I am hoping that after more than two decades of performing, Sobule is going to be an overnight sensation.

February 2, 2003

Is Lucian Freud Hot?

His paintings ask: Is this all there is?

British painter Lucian Freud is considered Britain's greatest living painter, one of the towering figures of realist portraiture. The largest retrospective of Freud's work has now come to Los Angeles's Museum of Contemporary Art (MOCA), the only US venue for this exhibit.

Organized in 2002 for the Tate Britain in London, this show gathers Freud's work over six decades—paintings, watercolors, drawings, as well as new works for this exhibition—a powerful testament to one painter's life's work. It is a demanding and challenging show. As I walked through the exhibit last week, I wondered, why LA? Why now?

The official reason is not particularly satisfying: "Freud's work has never really been shown in LA," said Rebecca Morse, the MOCA curatorial assistant who was kind enough to accompany me through the exhibit. Morse, who is thoughtful and articulate, feels that the exhibit itself makes a powerful case for Freud's artistry—his unsentimental look at the human body, the aging process, his choice of models, his compositions, even his changing use of paint across the years are distinctive elements in his art. True enough.

Freud's work, however, seems particularly compelling and relevant to our lives and to this moment in time. If you are not familiar with Freud's work, be forewarned: Most of the portraits in the exhibit are not pretty—some could even be considered ugly.

These are not Degas' pretty dancers, or Manet's nude *Olympia* or Ingres' *Odalisque*. Freud's paintings are about the body as animal. Young or old, clothed or nude, awake or in repose, emaciated or obese, the portraits are filled with defeat and desire, humans alive yet in a process of decay. The paintings of human shells saddled by their own corpulence are particularly striking—you stare, thinking as Shakespeare put it: "O, that this too, too solid flesh would melt."

Perhaps it is this display that makes Freud's work the perfect counterpoint to Los Angeles, a fleshpot so notorious that it dares to ask, as the philosopher Lorenzo Lamas put it so winningly the other night on TV: "Are you hot?"

Post September 11, we may also be more receptive to the art of the ugly. Freud's paintings offer a level of truth that resonates at a time when the culture is searching for the authentic, whether in Eminem's raps or in Nia Vardolos' *My Big Fat Greek Wedding*.

Freud has described his paintings to the critic William Feaver (the show's curator and Freud's biographer) as "factual not literal." They are meant to be as much of our time as Picasso's "ugly" painting, *Les Demoiselles D'Avignon*. Finally, in the wake of the trauma of terrorism and the gathering clouds of war, there is some comfort in the pictorial and the portrait, as opposed to the abstract or conceptual.

The Freud exhibit also reveals another question critical to the drama of our lives in LA: the tension between the surface existence and a life deeply observed. Freud's paintings dare us to ask: Is this all there is? Are Freud's paintings just compositions—arrangements of planes, colors, forms on a canvas, a true depiction of the people in his life and who cross over into his studio—or is there another dimension at work here. Is Freud's work—dare I say it—Freudian?

Not that this is an original thought: Freud has repeatedly denied any connection to his famous grandfather Sigmund Freud's work. He didn't really read the work, if at all, until late in his life. If Sigmund Freud's work is about the world of the mind, then the case can be made that Lucian Freud's is all about the body. Yet the connections are unavoidable.

"It's there for anyone to see," Thomas M. Brod of the LA Psychoanalytic Society and Institute told me recently. "Whether he disavows it or not. It's obvious and it's deep."

When Dr. Brod, who saw the Freud exhibit in London, heard it was coming to Los Angeles, he immediately called MOCA to organize two panels: one for analysts called "An Introduction to the Paintings of Lucian Freud," at the LA Psychoanalytic Auditorium; the other, "Lucian Freud: Psychoanalytic Look," at MOCA, at which various analysts will share their insights into Freud's life and work.

Dr. Brod pointed out that there are many details of Lucian Freud's life and his work to interest an analyst. For example, Sigmund Freud was his mother's favorite and was doted on by her. So, too, Lucian Freud. Lucian Freud was always regarded as special in his family—as an artist. Lucian Freud, commented Dr. Brod, "is a genius, whether he likes it or not."

In my conversation with Dr. Brod, I also noted that I was struck by the fact Freud is frequently referred to as "self-taught." In Feaver's biographical catalogue essay, Freud comments about his struggle to overcome his limitations and teach himself the necessary technique to paint his portraits.

As for Sigmund Freud, in matters of analysis, he, too, was self-taught (and self-analyzed), forced to come up with the technique to craft his "portraits" of his patients. At one level, both grandfather and grandson searched to render a great truth from their subjects.

For me, the connection appears even more evident: The edges of the painter's canvas are the same as the four walls of the analyst's room. Both concentrate on figures seated or reclining.

What occurs in the room, like what occurs on the canvas, is "the stuff"—the process that yields the work. Analysis is a conversation, painting, too, between subject and painter—and the results of what occurs in the room are destined for the outside world. The dynamic is remarkably similar. A Freud is a Freud.

Dr. Brad Collins has written extensively about psychoanalysis and art, particularly in the works of Leonardo, Gauguin and Degas. Sigmund Freud, Dr. Collins commented, wasn't able to discuss what makes an art work beautiful. But psychoanalysis can address content and the choices an artist makes in his work.

An analyst may choose to go where art historians fear to tread. As an example, Dr. Collins suggested that an analyst might see Freud's fleshy figures as enveloping the spectator, much in the same way an infant views his parents. However, Freud rejects all these analyses, explaining that his paintings are organized as formal compositions.

When I recently visited the exhibit, Morse pointed to one painting in which a pair of legs appears under a bed. Freud has explained that he just decided that worked best for that composition. But that is hard to believe: We all know that sometimes there are more than two people in a bed, and that who's under the bed is as important as who's in the bed.

The Freud exhibit gathers together 110 oil canvases arranged in chronological order. It is their cumulative effect that makes the exhibit's psychological dimension so overwhelming. It is hard not to be struck by the shadow of depression hovering over the work.

Although there are moments of iridescent brightness within the works, the overall palette seems gray. You can blame the London light or the weather, but it seems to go beyond that. And of course, if we are discussing Freud, Sigmund or Lucian, we need to talk about the mother.

In 1972, Freud began painting his mother. His father had died in 1970, and his mother had become severely depressed.

Feaver notes that Freud brought her to his studio to keep an eye on her and continued to do so four or five days a week, until the mid-1980s. Immobilized by her depression, she began to sit for Freud.

Here's what Freud says: "She barely noticed, but I had to overcome a lifetime of avoiding her. From very early on, she treated me, in a way, as an only child. I resented her interest; I felt it was threatening. She was so intuitive. And she liked forgiving me; she forgave me for things I never did."

'Nuff said? One need not be a Freud to get this.

"My work is purely autobiographical. It is about myself and my surroundings." This is the maxim that greets visitors to the MOCA exhibit.

We meet Freud's friends, his lovers, his mother, his children, his bookie, among others passing through his studio. Freud's work may be viewed as violent, brutal, portraits where even the passive and depressed are treated with aggression.

There are also several self-portraits: Freud depicts himself as he ages unsentimentally but ferociously. The brushstrokes in these portraits speak volumes: It is as if Freud's paint were a life force itself, raging against death.

As for Freud's connection to his famous last name, one can argue that Freud, like many if not most people, spent the first half of his life trying to distinguish himself and the second half making peace with who he'd become. But it does not answer whether a famous last name is a blessing, a curse or both. Does it determine who you are and what you do? That's a question Saddam Hussein will probably never get to ask President George W. Bush.

In the meantime, Freud has brought his intense analysis of the way of all flesh to challenge us. The retrospective gives lie to Freud's claim that his paintings are just "factual" formal compositions.

If they were, they would be no more compelling than wallpaper. Freud does not merely chronicle his life or paint his friends—he uses them to analyze (there's that Sigmund again!) his life and our times.

What makes Freud's paintings so enthralling and so relevant to our lives here in paradise is the drama just below the surface, a battle between who we strive to be and who we become, between our parents and ourselves, between our minds and our bodies, between life and death.

Freud, like his grandfather, asks: Are we just bodies?

The answer is to look closer. Whether we are talking about Sigmund Freud or Lucian Freud, we certainly can agree: If the unexamined life isn't worth living, it certainly isn't worth painting. Even on "Are You Hot?" No one is a perfect ten (at least not yet).

February 28, 2003

Is Hollywood Against the War?

Across the country, Americans are wondering, "Why is Hollywood against the war?"

On TV programs and TV and radio talk shows, in magazines and newspapers, they see actors and actresses opining, talking the talk and walking the anti-war walk. This has led to a separate thread of programs and opinion pieces about whether Hollywood stars should even be called upon to discuss national issues. Around and around it goes.

I can't speak for Hollywood. But from where I sit, here in *Tommywood*, the true nature of this discourse seems obvious. Like so much in our culture, it is about ratings.

As our president put it so eloquently in a recent press conference, "Nobody likes war." It's natural. Most people are reluctant to engage in armed battle and cause grievous harm to our own and to others.

I've been studying Civil War history recently, and we weren't so enthusiastic about that war on our own soil. Many times, even during the course of the Civil War, there was pressure on President Lincoln to get out.

Americans were reluctant to enter World War I. We didn't rush into World War II either. Pearl Harbor, as Jerry Bruckheimer and Michael Bay instructed us, brought us into a battle we had been avoiding. So let's just say there is a natural reluctance to enter war.

This natural reluctance is given all the more reason to vent because our president has done a poor job of rallying the world, as well as our citizens, to his cause. Case in point: After September 11, you didn't see a lot of complaining about going into Afghanistan (some, but not a lot).

But in a situation where the president must argue by alluding to "secret evidence"; talking about stocks of weapons that have disappeared, rather than showing us actual weapons of mass destruction; where he must convince us to engage in what is now being called a "pre-emptive" war, that feeds the natural ambivalence.

But back to the original point: why is Hollywood perceived as being against the war?

For the most part it's because a small number of celebrities appearing on TV and radio can garner a disproportionate amount of attention.

Producer Robert Greenwald, co-chair with actor Mike Farrell of Artists for Winning Without War, gives a rough estimate that their group of more than 100 celebrities has been able to reach more than 120 million people with their anti-war message through traditional and nontraditional media (i.e., entertainment shows and magazines). The artists include a wide range of talents going literally from A to Z—from Gillian Anderson to Howard Zinn.

"Our goal," Greenwald says, "was not to change peoples' minds. Our goal, with the disappearance [post-September 11] of any opposition, was to get attention for another point of view."

In that, Greenwald believes they have been successful.

When he started the organization last fall, dissent was deemed not "patriotic." Today, he believes that more and more people are comfortable expressing their opposition to a "pre-emptive" war.

By contrast, Hollywood celebrities who support the war have been relatively absent from the media. Some, like Tom Cruise and Steven Spielberg, have expressed support for regime change in Iraq, but many more have remained silent.

Sandy Frank, a co-producer on the political drama *Mr. Sterling*, believes that conservatives in Hollywood are in such a distinct minority that they are afraid, or know better, than to speak out. The problem, as Frank sees it, is that "conservatives think liberals are wrong, but liberals think conservatives are evil." Nonetheless, the majority of TV and radio talk show hosts are conservative, and they all want one thing: higher ratings.

Who is making the case that Hollywood is against the war?

It is the celebrity-driven newsmagazines. It is the conservative commentators in the press, on radio and TV who, for the most part, are not really journalists—they are entertainers. They would prefer to "debate" celebrities than engage in discussion with political scientists, politicians and foreign affairs correspondents.

There are many important academics both in this country and in Europe who have their misgivings about this war. There are foreign policy experts who believe in containment or who argue for greater coalition building.

I will not make their arguments for them. However, if you want to hear their opinions, you can watch *Charlie Rose*. Harvard professor Stanley Hoffman, for example, appeared recently to talk about his deep misgivings about America's Iraq policy. But that is public television. You won't find Hoffman on *Hannity & Colmes.*

Which brings me to another point. Walk by a newsstand. What sells magazines?

Celebrities. We know it; the TV and radio programs know it, and guess what? The celebrities know it, too. So there is a dance whereby the shows want the celebrities who have opinions they know they can express that might not be heard otherwise.

The shows are only too happy to oblige them so they can have their cake and eat it, too: they can benefit from the improved ratings, and then dismiss the celebrities as nitwits if they so chose.

How does Israel calculate into this arithmetic?

Although there is every reason to believe that war with Iraq could mean Iraqi attacks on Israel, the global anti-American brigades are filled with friends they saw the week before at anti-Israel protests. This was brought to light in a recent Wall Street Journal Op-Ed piece by Tikkun's Michael Lerner, who found himself banned from speaking at a peace rally in San Francisco, because Lerner, who despite being a vocal critic of the Sharon government, was deemed, "too pro-Israel."

By contrast Hollywood may be one of the few places one can be proudly pro-Israel and anti-war. Is that a reason for Hollywood to support the war or be against it?

I called Rabbi Steven Carr Reuben of Kehillat Israel in Pacific Palisades, whose congregation represents a cross-section of Hollywood, to discuss this topic. Reuben recalled that he came of age protesting the war in Vietnam. Yet, now he feels ambivalence about protesting this incursion. And he feels his ambivalence is shared by his congregation.

But the rabbi told me he will not protest this war; he will support it. He feels he has no choice, because of Saddam.

"Recently we mourned Ilan Ramon," Reuben said of the Israeli astronaut who perished in the shuttle disaster. "Ramon was a hero because he participated in the Israeli air attack on Iraq's Osiris [nuclear] reactor."

As the rabbi pointed out, that was a pre-emptive strike against Saddam. How can we oppose one now?

So, is Hollywood actually against the war?

Of course not. Hollywood is filled with people who are for, against and, for the most part, ambivalent—like the rest of the country. But the reasons for ambivalence and for support of a war, if and when it happens, are equally obvious: 1. Saddam Hussein is a bad guy; 2. We know that if he gets access to weapons of mass destruction, he will use them; 3. There is no scenario under which a year from now he is a better guy.

In the end, we may feel about going to war, as the Economist put it so memorably, "Saddamned, perhaps, if you do; but Saddamned, also, if you don't."

That may not be a reason to go to war, but it is reason enough to support one. As no doubt Hollywood will do. But don't take my word for it, you'll read all about in *People* magazine.

March 14, 2003

Polanski Hits a Sour Note in *Pianist*

Truth to tell, I didn't start to despise *The Pianist*—Roman's Polanski's Oscar-nominated film of concert pianist Wladyslaw Szpilman's memoirs of Warsaw during World War II—until the very end of the film: The war has ended and a friend has taken Szpilman to a farm in the Polish countryside. There used to be a Soviet POW camp there, where the Nazi officer who spared Szpilman was asking for him. Now there is no trace of that internment camp.

When the movie ends, a title card informs us that the Nazi, Wilm Hosenfeld, died in a Soviet camp in 1952.

It is a strange scene and epilogue. For some, this demonstrates the arbitrariness of war; the Nazi hoped that helping a Jew would pay off—it didn't.

But for me, this sequence was far more troubling. When I think of a small farm in Poland set up to hide the existence of a camp that used to be there, I don't think of a Soviet prisoner of war camp.

What comes to mind is Treblinka. After the 1943 uprising, the Nazis razed the camp, plowed the land and set up a farmer in a farmhouse so that no one would know the terrible secret of the more than 870,000 murders that took place there in little over a year—murders that included Szpilman's brothers and sisters, his parents and most of Warsaw's Jews. Yet there is no title card to tell us the fate of Szpilman's family.

Is Polanski saying that the Soviets were as bad as the Nazis? I say Polanski (and his screenwriter Ronald Harwood) and not Szpilman, because the title card about Hosenfeld is not part of Szpilman's memoir. Szpilman's memoir ends with his freedom in Warsaw and a visit to a suburb where he sees a human skeleton and mourns that "there are no such remains of my sisters, beautiful Regina and youthful, serious Halina, and I shall never find a grave where I could pray for their souls."

That sentiment Polanski chose not to include. I find the choice reprehensible.

Szpilman does add a postscript describing the visit to search for the German officer whose name he never knew and whom he hopes is safe. Szpilman describes Hosenfeld this way: "The one human being that I met wearing German uniform." That distinction is also one that the film does not honor.

Polanski's moral relativism is also shared by Szpilman's son. The Picador paperback edition of *The Pianist* includes a foreword by Szpilman's son, who writes, "I've lived in Germany for many years, and I am always conscious of the painful absence of communication between the Jews and the Germans and the Poles. I hope this book will help to close some of the wounds that are still open."

So whose movie is this anyway?

My objection to *The Pianist* is not about whether it is a good Holocaust movie or not. To the extent it is true to Szpilman's memoir, it can't be faulted. Szpilman's feelings about Hosenfeld are understandable in the context of what he endured.

Today we call it "Stockholm Syndrome," where prisoners begin to feel so grateful to their captors for any kindness that they come to venerate them. Just ask Patty Hearst or Elizabeth Smart. But that does not excuse Polanski, who, I feel, has a much larger agenda.

The Pianist is not so much Szpilman's story as it is Polanski's apologia for his life. Polanski has said that he could never film the story of his own survival—that would be too much to bear. But to the extent *The Pianist* is about Polanski, I find the movie to be meretricious in the extreme.

Basically, Polanski's *Pianist* makes the case that we should cut artists a break. Throughout the movie, Szpilman is granted special consideration, because he is a *Pianist*: his parents get work passes, a Jewish policeman pulls him off the train bound for Treblinka, non-Jewish co-workers from the radio station hide him and introduce him to other Poles who feed and shelter him, until finally a German officer spares him after hearing Szpilman play for him. Szpilman's survival, it turns out, is not random. It is because he is an artist.

This is also the story of Polanski's life. Although born in Paris, Polanski was a child in Krakow when the war began. Separated from his parents, he survived the Holocaust hidden in the countryside by non-Jews (he spent some time literally escaping in movie houses).

After the war, he was reunited with his father (his mother died in Auschwitz), became a child actor and was later accepted at the Lodz film school. Polanski's status as an actor and then a film director afforded him a better life under the Communists.

Being a film director allowed him to leave Poland and work in England. Being a film director brought him to Hollywood and afforded him a lifestyle known only to a few. And finally, being an artist has allowed him asylum in Europe under circumstances that surely would have meant extradition back to the United States for nonartists.

The parallels go further: Szpilman experiences bombs falling on Warsaw, the start of the war, the arrival of the Germans and many events, including the Warsaw Ghetto uprising, the attack on the German police headquarters, even the Germans' eventual withdrawal from Warsaw and the arrival of the Russians—all from behind a pane of glass.

In a similar fashion, Polanski, as a director, has also spent most of his life behind a lens. Even the notorious incident leading to the charge of statutory rape has always been described as something that occurred during a photo shoot.

Which brings me to my final comments: We know that the Holocaust did not discriminate among Jews—religious, nonreligious, rich, poor, all were subject to fate. Artists were given no special breaks.

Recent publications about the work of Bruno Schulz and a current exhibit on art created in death camps (at The Jewish Museum in New York) make clear that the artistic impulse survived during the war, even as the artists themselves were murdered. Polanski has chosen to adapt Szpilman's Holocaust memoir, and with that I have no quibble.

Schindler's List which, for better or worse has become a reference point in any discussion of films of this era, provides an important contrast. Although there are many reasons to critique the film, in *Schindler's List*, Spielberg put his ego aside and used everything he knew about filmmaking, every trick in his bag, to make the most compelling film possible.

Polanski's *The Pianist* is just the opposite: In the end, it fails because it is all about Polanski's ego.

Polanski has remained in Europe rather than face American Justice for a crime that he does not dispute he committed. He asks the sentence be mitigated because he is an artist. He remains abroad because he fears the argument will fail in an American court.

In my opinion, it has failed on film as well.

March 21, 2003

No Laughing Matter

Calvin Trillin, Peter Lefcourt and the comic novel

Over the last year, I have read many wonderful novels: *The Lovely Bones* by Alice Sebold, *Atonement* by Ian McEwan, *The Hours* by Michael Cunningham. Well-written, emotionally resonant, all bestsellers, these highly praised literary works are required reading in book groups in Los Angeles and across the nation. Yet as excellent as they were, as one critic said of *Schindler's List*: "There weren't that many laughs."

By contrast, *Tepper Isn't Going Out* by Calvin Trillin delivers more pleasure, more belly laughs per page than any other work in recent memory.

Tepper Isn't Going Out is the story of Murray Tepper, a New Yorker who has survived many mayoral regimes and has passed through the many stages of parking life in New York City, from metered, to alternate side of the street, to garaged parking a few blocks from his apartment. Suddenly, Tepper decides to spend his time sitting in his car, reading the newspaper at desirable metered parking spots around the city.

People, friends, family, passersby start asking him why? His answers are always literal: "Because there's still time on the meter."

Quoting Trillin's phrases out of context does not do them comic justice. Suffice to say, paraphrasing A. J. Libeling's appraisal of his own talents: "There is no humor writer who can write better and no better writer who can write more humorously."

Trillin has been funny for a long time, most famously chronicling his adventures in eating for *The New Yorker*. He has written about almost every aspect of his life—except explaining how Calvin came to be a Jewish name (something we might also ask Mr. Klein—but I digress). Still, *Tepper* is fiction, and it presents an exquisite achievement.

Yet *Tepper* has won no Pulitzer, National Book Award, nor Jewish Book Award. And why not?

I have a simple answer: because funny gets no respect. I suppose this is true in the film world as well, where studios gripe that comedies and comic performances are rarely nominated for Academy Awards—but at least there we know that funny is money and popularity is some consolation.

To discuss the difficulties inherent in the comic novel, I called up a local practitioner of this neglected art, Peter Lefcourt. Lefcourt has written such very funny and brilliant works as *Di and I*, *The Dreyfus Affair*, and *The Woody*.

His touch is light and deft—*The Dreyfus Affair* has more to say about macho and politics in professional sports than any three sports columnists combined. (He also has published a new memoir of loves past in the form of a novel, *Eleven Karens*.)

Publishers are not big fans of comic fiction, Lefcourt believes, because the novels "don't always translate well into foreign languages" (so no large foreign sales). Humor is often a matter of individual taste, and comic novels often appeal to a "small and select audience."

We also discussed how many of the funniest fiction appears in short stories and how hard it is to sustain comedy in a novel. "Comic fiction is largely a matter of understatement," Lefcourt said.

He's right, of course. There are many people who can tell or even write a joke, and a few can put together a stand-up or a monologue. There are those who can write a brilliant sitcom, but how many of them have written humorous novels?

Woody Allen has written short stories. Steve Martin has written a collection of humor pieces, but his novel, *Shopgirl*, was more serious. NPR has fostered a collection of new humorists, such as David and Amy Sedaris, Sarah Vowel and Ian Brown, but again, they work the short form.

Perhaps the greatest miniaturist was S. J. Perelman. Today, Perelman is mostly known as the co-author of some Marx Brothers movies and Oscar-winner for *Around the World in 80 Days*, but he was a hilarious and impeccable stylist, whose motto was, "Misery breeds copy."

As for recent comic novels, *A Year in Provence* made for a pleasant afternoon, and *Le Divorce* was fairly irresistible. I barreled though *The Nanny Diaries* and *Bridget Jones' Diary,* as well as all of Nick Hornby's novels.

I highly recommend Peter Farrelly's novel, *The Comedy Writer*, but it's a shame that his success with *There's Something About Mary*" seems to be distracting him from his true calling.

Still none match the comic timing and rate of laughs per page as Trillin.

What, as the Bolsheviks used to say, is to be done? In publishing, it seems comic fiction presents a devil's bargain: People will enjoy your work, but few will ever admit it. Sales will be modest, praise faint.

Maybe humor is a hothouse flower that they are afraid will wither if nourished. I suggest the Pulitzer committee create a new fiction award not for seriousness of intent but for laughs per page. As the Romans were fond of pointing out: Art is long, but life is short.

A good laugh is not always easy to come by and deserves high praise. Consider it a much-needed tonic for our times. Viva *Tepper*! Viva Trillin!

April 4, 2003

Hungarians in Hollywood

When my friend Lawrence Karman, cameraman par excellence, invited me a few weeks ago to a screening of *Bánk Bán*, the filmed version of the classic Hungarian nationalist opera, I accepted enthusiastically. Not because I'm a big fan of opera in general or Hungarian operas in particular, but rather because it would give Larry and I an opportunity to wax nostalgic about our favorite subject: Hungarians in Hollywood.

There was a time in the 1930s and 1940s, the story goes, that a billboard was posted at the border of Hollywood: "It's not enough to be Hungarian, you also have to have talent."

Those were the days when Michael Curtiz of *Casablanca* fame, was known as Mihály Kertész, former head of the Budapest film studios. Adolf Zukor and Bill Fox were in the first wave of Magyars to colonize Hollywood but they were soon joined by many other countrymen. Bela Lugosi kept his accent, Leslie Howard didn't and Peter Lorre had an accent of his own invention. Back then, Zoltan Kordan might direct a film, Vincent Korda would do the sets and Sir Alexander Korda would produce it. Screenplay by Ferenc Molnár, score by Miklos Roza. Card games abounded, filled with refugees from the

Austro-Hungarian empire under whose umbrella we might find such diverse talents as Paul Muni, Billy Wilder, and Ernst Lubitsch.

Lawrence (or Latzi as I call him on such occasions) and I come by our Magyarphilia honestly. Our mothers were in high school together—in Budapest. We grew up with a touch of paprika in our blood and occasionally mourn for the vanished world.

Our soirée Hongroise began with dinner at Csardas, the Hungarian restaurant on Melrose near Vine. This is where we go to eat our soul food—cold cherry soup, wiener schnitzel, roast duck, some cucumber salad (all in large portions)—and speak the few words of Hungarian we remember to waiters who are always curious to know how anyone else could know their language. The Csardas recently installed a giant plasma screen with a satellite hookup so we watched live Hungarian TV as we overate.

We then made our way to a Hollywood Boulevard movie palace that has become a USC screening room. No sooner had we taken our seats than we heard the familiar chirping of aged Hungarians. More than two hours later as the credits rolled, I had heard more Hungarian than I had in ages and watched with delight as names such as Ildiko, Sandor, Ferenc, Istvan and Szabo scrolled before my eyes. Although I can't recommend the film on its own merits, for me it was fabulous—or as they are wont to say in Budapest, "fantasztik." After the screening, Vilmos Zsigmond, *Bánk Bán*'s cinematographer, held a Q-and-A. Just listening to his accent was a treat.

There was a time when being a Hungarian was a profession, a way of life. Being Hungarian, male or mogul version, combined a certain worldliness with an ability to walk the thin line between what was black and white to others, savoring life's pleasures and delighting in the ironies inherent in one's place in the world (Jack Nicholson must have some Hungarian blood in him!). This was best illustrated in Michael Korda's biography of his uncle Alexander, *Charmed Lives*, which I recommend enthusiastically.

On the distaff side, need we say more than Zsa Zsa? The Gabor girls were certainly one of Hungary's more famous exports. At a time when American women had Betty Crocker, June Cleaver and Donna Reed as their ideals, the Gabors were women whose femininity and wit empowered them as the masters of their own fate. They were beautiful, sexy, worldly and no one's fool. Although caricatured as gold diggers, they were smart businesswomen whose fortunes were self-made and not, as popularly believed, a product of marriage settlements.

The overwhelming majority of the Hungarians in Hollywood from the 1930s and 1940s were Jewish, whether they knew it or not. My mother used to say that she knew the Gabors so long ago that she knew them when they were Jewish. As the 1999 movie *Sunshine* portrayed so movingly, Budapest's Jewish middle and upper class were assimilated and never believed that the Nazis and Hungarian fascists would treat them as Hitler had treated the Polish Jews. Those fortunate enough to escape remained citizens of the world. They would face the world and their Judaism on their own terms, not Hitler's. Many have tried to explain the ambition, restlessness and charm of the Hungarians to no avail. As Nobel physicist Enrico Fermi said when asked if he believed in extraterrestrials: "They are here...and they are called Hungarians."

Today, few professional Hungarians abound. There's Robert Halmi of Hallmark Entertainment fame, *Terminator* producer Andy Vajna and Robert Lantos, a very successful Canadian TV and film producer. The 1956 Revolution gave Hollywood Vilmos Zsigmond and the equally celebrated cinematographer, Lazlo Kovacs. More recently, the Hungarian with the greatest impact on popular culture is probably Budapest-born Gabor Csupo, who, with his partner Arlene Klasky, has given us *Rugrats* and *The Wild Thornberrys*, among many other animated programs that I watch devotedly with my daughter.

Finally, there are the children of the immigrant—sons and daughters—who like me, can curse the most convoluted profanities in our mother tongue but have trouble saying much else. In other words, Tony Curtis, Gene Simmons, Tommy Ramone, Mark Knopfler, Brent Spiner, Mariska Hargitay, and Rachel Weisz would all know a palacinta (blintz) if they saw one.

Odon Kiraly of the Hungarian Consulate estimates there are 70,000 Hungarians in California with the overwhelming majority in the Los Angeles area. Where are they? Will there be a new wave? I hope so. I dream of Larry and I, after a hard day's work, leaving a sound stage on the Paramount lot, turning to the rest of the actors and crew, and waving as we shout to each the farewell known far and wide in Hollywood and Budapest and by my daughter as well, "Servusz!"

April 18, 2003

DYLAN IS THE KEY TO *MASKED* LA

Masked and Anonymous is a new movie starring Bob Dylan that premiered at Sundance. Director Larry Charles has described his film as an "apocalyptic spaghetti noir western." No surprise: The reviews were not kind.

Nonetheless, *Masked and Anonymous* is a great title. It seems the perfect phrase to describe Dylan, even as a metaphor for his many personas over the years. At the same time, it is also a great metaphor for the city of Los Angeles and the lives we lead in it.

Until I started thinking about *Masked and Anonymous,* I never realized how intertwined Dylan is with Los Angeles.

When we think of Dylan, the New York folk scene comes to mind: Greenwich Village, where he first played and later lived, and Minnesota, from where he hails, or even "the road" of his never-ending tour.

But the truth is Los Angeles is Dylan's home. It is where he has lived longer than anywhere else. It is where his ex-wives live, where his children were raised and where several of his children and grandchildren now live. It is where he boxes, where he davens. He is of Los Angeles.

My one encounter with Dylan took place here in Los Angeles several years ago. It was lunch time, and I was waiting to meet a friend on the back porch of the House of Blues. The door opened, and there I stood face to face with Dylan.

It was a hot day, and Dylan was wearing some sort of multicolored suit that looked more like the upholstery on a chair than everyday wear. His skin was pasty, and he had on dark glasses.

I looked at him, and he looked at me. And in the awkward way one does when you can't have the conversation you always wanted to have, I thanked him for all the pleasure and companionship his music had given me over the years.

He didn't say anything. Then I held out my hand, and he gave the limp-fish handshake, which was a disappointment—and he was gone.

But that is very much Los Angeles. Random run-ins with the great, the near-great and the ingrate. A town where you decide what you want to wear by how you feel, rather than what the weather is.

Sean Wilentz, the historian in residence at BobDylan.com (he's also a professor of history at Princeton), feels there are several ways in which Dylan's work is very expressive of Los Angeles. First of all, Dylan is of the West, and the West and its mythology has always been important to him.

Second is the importance of the movies in his work. Ever since he was a teenager, Dylan has been fascinated by the movies and by movie stars. Now he is very much a part of Hollywood. He's received a Grammy as well as an Oscar (for best song on *Wonder Boys*) and seemed genuinely pleased to have done so.

More important is that Dylan's songs are cinematic in their imagery. By way of example, Wilentz cites Dylan's album *Desire* as filled with minimovies, such as *One More Cup of Coffee.* "The movies have played a great role in Dylan's imaginative life," Wilentz said.

I've lived in Los Angeles for almost a decade now. When I first visited in the late 1970s, I kept asking, "Where's the city?" When I first drove my mother around the mansions of Beverly Hills, she asked, "Where are all the people?"

When friends would come to visit, it was hard to know where to take them to show them Los Angeles. I used to laugh about how real estate brokers sold homes by telling you who lived there and extolling the air (as in "the air is so much better on the Westside"), but Los Angeles is all about the light, the sun, the air, the people, the movies, the quality of life as it slips through your fingers.

Dylan may well be the poet laureate of our inner lives in this city. For its part, Los Angeles, like Dylan, is masked and anonymous, waiting for each of us to discover it.

May 16, 2003

Affirmative Actions

A Place Called Home; The Accelerated School; P.S. ARTS

If you want to talk about education, if you want to discuss affirmative action, you need to take a trip with me down the 10 Freeway. Let's head east past the 405 and the 110 and exit on Central Avenue, heading south. That's right—South Central, recently renamed South Los Angeles.

Driving on Central Avenue, you get inured to a certain version of urban neglect—you begin to take gang tagging as a given. Then you come to A Place Called Home (APCH)—a gleaming white building at 29th Street and South Central Avenue. There's no graffiti there. That's the first sign of community respect you see at APCH. But there's more inside.

APCH is a safe harbor for nine- to twenty-year-olds. Started as an after-school program, APCH now includes a Los Angeles Unified School District-certified public school for those who've either missed forty-five days of school and are not allowed to return to their schools, been asked to leave school or been assigned to APCH's school by the courts.

If I were pitching this to a studio, I might describe it as *Lean On Me* meets *Fame*. There's a dance program and a computer lab where students can improve their skills or even be trained to receive certification as a computer technician. There are two music studios where students can play, sing and perform, as well as have group and private music lessons.

There are yoga classes, martial arts, and a gym with serious workout machines. There's a lunch area where healthy meals are served. There are counselors for both children and their parents, offering gang prevention and interventions, as well as drug and alcohol treatment.

There is food and clothing distribution for the community, as well as Medi-Cal enrollment. There is a library where they don't loan books, they give them away.

Here's what they don't have at APCH: no gang colors, no gang signs, no drugs, no guns, no violence. The school has a higher attendance and graduation rate than the local public school. And it all began with one woman: Debrah Constance.

Constance is the founder and the president of APCH—it is her mission and her dream. She's the former Jon Douglas executive who gave up a lucrative career to create a safe haven for children in South Central.

Rabbi Jan Goldstein's new book, *Sacred Wounds*, tells in great detail of the journey that brought Constance, a high school dropout and recovering alcoholic, to found APCH in 1994 to help children whom so many others had given up on. (APCH was also profiled in *The Journal* in July 2000.)

Constance started in May 1993 with twelve children in two rooms of a church. Today, APCH works with 4,800 children, has forty-four employees and an annual budget of 1.6 million dollars. Despite generous funds from a combination of corporate support and individuals, including Jasmine Guy, Johnny

Carson, Will and Jada Pinkett Smith, Colin Horowitz, Rick Wisely, and Steve Winston, APCH survives month to month and is in desperate need of greater support.

When you first walk into APCH, it is at the same time low-key and overwhelming. Some of the kids are scary looking—or rather they've been schooled in the art of intimidation—until they start smiling at you, which they all seem to do.

Don't ever think that one person can't make a difference: It's hard to walk around APCH and not be moved by what one woman has accomplished.

But what about younger children who are all dreams and potential?

A few minutes away at the corner of Martin Luther King Boulevard and Main Street is The Accelerated School (TAS), a public charter school with the soul and vibe of the best private schools. TAS currently educates 360 children, K-8, with plans to expand a class a year until it can offer a K-12 school.

TAS is the school that its founders, Jonathan Williams and Kevin Sved, dreamed of as teachers at South Central's 99th Street Elementary School. At TAS, every child is treated as gifted; children can get all the tutoring they need to keep up—but there is no getting around meeting the school's rigorous standards. Students and parents both sign a contract that mandates their involvement in the school.

TAS was founded in 1994 (based on Dr. Henry Levin of Stanford University's model program) and began with 50 students, grades K-4, operating out of the community rooms of St. Stephen's Church. They had to put away the classrooms Friday and reassemble them after Sunday school.

When Williams and Sved received a 200,000 dollar grant from Wells Fargo, they knew their dream had a chance. However Williams and Sved's big break came when fashion designer Carole Little and her husband and business partner, Leonard Rabinowitz, were considering donating their headquarters and warehouse in South Central to an educational institution.

Little and Rabinowitz entrusted the decision to Tara Lynda Guber, who at the time was president of Education First! Guber's decision to support TAS (she is now on the board) and the donation of the building (which was valued at over six million dollars) took the school to a whole other level. Guber then pledged to raise the necessary funds so that they could one day tear down the Carole Little building and construct their own dream facility, one that would house a K-12 school. That school will open in September in an award-winning building designed by architects Marmol, Radziner + Associates.

Guber, who is also a well-known yoga figure, has introduced yoga as a physical education elective at TAS—and I say this to skeptics: watching a group of awkward nine-year-olds find grace and calm doing yoga poses was one of the surprise pleasures of my recent tour of TAS.

The students at TAS wear uniforms (a parent-led decision) of light-blue polo shirts with the school's name on it and dark-blue shorts, pants or skirts. There is no screening for admitting students—it's done by lottery.

However, because this is a charter school, it is not bound by union regulations for teachers and it can dismiss students who breach their contracts. The net result is a highly motivated group of students, parents and teachers. There is currently a waiting list of 2,000 for the school, which hopes to be the model for other charter schools in Los Angeles and around the country.

TAS provides opportunity for the motivated child; A Place Called Home is a safe harbor and second chance for what Constance calls "the children no one wants."

However, my inner seder leader asks, what about the everyday children? The children who attend public schools in low-income neighborhoods, the innocent victims of budget cuts and the elimination of arts programs. Is anyone reaching out to them?

I'm glad you asked. Let me to tell you about P.S. Arts.

P.S. Arts was founded in 1991 by Paul Cummins, the former Crossroads (private school) headmaster, with seed money from Herb Alpert. Their mission was to restore arts education to underserved public schools in Los Angeles.

They began by focusing on the 450 students of the Broadway Elementary School in Venice-Westchester area, providing them with an hour of musical and visual arts education a week. Fourth- and fifth-graders received drama instruction, while others were offered dance.

Today, they reach almost 6,000 students in more than a dozen schools. In addition, P.S. Arts provides students with field trips to museums, theaters and galleries, guest artists, after-school programs and arranges professional development workshops for teachers.

I recently visited the Grand View Elementary School (near Grand View Boulevard and Washington Place), where P.S. Arts has donated an "arts bungalow." What that really means is a two-room building it paid for and installed. One is a music room.

On the day I visited, a group of 30 kids were preparing a performance. Half the class played individual xylophones, while a quarter danced and the other quarter read from a text relating to their American history studies. The kids were shy, embarrassed and totally delighted.

Next door, Tamie Smith, a very high-energy art teacher, was inspiring thirty fifth-graders to illustrate thought bubbles. The students were working on their own in groups of twos and threes.

As Smith pointed out, at the beginning of the term, some of the students were not speaking English—some of the Mexican children didn't even speak Spanish (they spoke Zapotec)—and they were now expressing their feelings through art. Not bad for a day's work.

P.S. Arts does not happen in a vacuum. It is fortunate to have the indefatigable Laurie David spearheading its board, a very committed staff, exceptional volunteers and a very active board of trustees (of which my wife is a member). But as budget cuts increase, P.S. Arts is needed more than ever.

Caring about education is why I was heading down the 10 in the first place (not as some may suspect to have lunch at a certain Creole eatery on Slauson Avenue—although I did manage to slip in a little Yucatan chicken from Chicken Itza at the Mercado de la Paloma).

Let me set this story in context: The last week in March is when private schools in Los Angeles send out their verdicts. The Geneva marriage convention prohibits me from offering the actual details of my daughter's kindergarten application process.

However, suffice to say, the decision of where to send our child—to private or public, to secular or parochial, to a developmental or academic school—for me was like walking into a maze of my own ambivalence. I was forced to consider the choices that my parents and I had made about my own education, the dreams and desires I have for my daughter (my projections) versus my weak-minded attempt to respect the person she is and will become (while trying not to be influenced by which school's parents I would most enjoy hanging with).

I pondered all this as if I had any say in the matter. As with most events in my life, the outcome was obvious from the start to everyone but me. But I digress.

The following week, the US Supreme Court heard arguments in the University of Michigan case regarding affirmative action. I've always believed that affirmative action is just an "old boys network" for people who don't have one.

Not everyone at the schools I went to got in because of their grades, test scores or personal essays. Some got in because of their siblings, parents, last names, or because of donations given or promised. No level playing field for them. (And why should there be? It's their name on the field.) Apparently, the families of legacies and donors recognize the value of having their children attend certain institutions—so why shouldn't the Supreme Court?

What I learned on my journey is that Los Angeles is filled with people who care deeply about education and who have chosen to do something to improve education for all students.

In the last decade, a group of—for the most part—high-achieving Westside women with potent Hollywood connections have taken it upon themselves to improve public education in Los Angeles. Could this happen in any city in the United States? Perhaps, but Los Angeles is uniquely populated with people who have the time, energy, talent, creativity, dedication and access to financial resources to accomplish it.

Maybe there's an element of guilt for the gilded lives we lead. So what? What is remarkable is their accomplishments, their affirmative actions. Why did I say theirs? They can be yours, too.

If you are interested in learning more about the institutions or organizations mentioned in this article, they could use your time, energy, ideas and/or financial support. Check out A Place Called Home at www.apch.org; The Accelerated School, www.accelerated.org., and P.S. Arts, psarts.org

May 23, 2003

Delightful Offensiveness Key to *Producers* Genius

To understand something of the success of *The Producers*, it helps to understand something of its history. There is probably no person on the planet who doesn't know the story of how this sensation of a musical came to pass, but let me quickly recap: In the early sixties, Mel Brooks writes the book for the Charles Strouse-Lee Adams musical *All American*. Their last musical *Bye Bye Birdie* was a hit. *All American* was not. Brooks wonders: *What if it was intentional?* From that germ of an idea, and a character Brooks worked for briefly after World War II, came the movie, *The Producers*.

This movie about a flop that becomes a hit followed a similar trajectory: the studio was so convinced the film was unmarketable that it sat on the shelf, the story goes, until Peter Sellers screened it and called it the funniest movie he'd ever seen. The movie was released and Brooks won an Oscar for the screenplay. That was in 1968. More than thirty years later, Brooks gets a call from David Geffen who insists it become a musical. Brooks tries to say no, but who says no to David Geffen? Thank God Geffen didn't call about *Spaceballs*.

In the end, so many producers came aboard that Geffen stepped aside. Sometimes being smarter than everyone else is reward enough. The overwhelmingly talented Susan Stroman joined the creative team as director-choreographer; William Ivey Long did the costumes; Robin Wagner the sets. Brooks (with Thomas Meehan) wrote the book and Brooks, himself, wrote more than ttwenty songs. The show was a smash and the rest is Tony history.

The irony is that by the turn of the millennium, Brooks had pretty much worn out his welcome in Hollywood. He had not had a hit in years, his humor seemed too old-fashioned and shticky and he had a maddening habit of inserting musical production numbers into his movies at a time when no one was interested in musicals. Go figure.

In spite of all this—and, at the same time, because of all this—*The Producers* became a success. The staging, the sets, the costumes, the choreography, the supporting roles, the show-girls—all great. The conceit of the show within a show, the flop that becomes a hit, became a hit. But that is not the main reason for its success: The whole production works because it is at the same time nostalgic and transgressive.

Transgressive is a word that I have always wanted to use in order to garner the attention and respect of academics. I'm not exactly sure what it means but I will tell you what I am referring to.

Brooks has created characters to bring tears of joy to any anti-Semite. The heroes, so called, are Max Bialystock, a theatrical producer who swindles old ladies out of their savings by seducing them (a cheat and a gigolo!), and Leo Bloom, a nebbish accountant who abandons his morals for the casting couch and finds his shiksa goddess in the ululating secretary-actress Ulla. Not to sound like Julius Streicher (or the punch line of one of my favorite jokes) but one could ask: What is it about you people and money? Yet I would venture to guess very few complaints have been lodged at the Anti-Defamation League and the Simon Wiesenthal Center.

There are many possible explanations. First and foremost, Brooks' exuberance in both being Jewish and making fun of Jews forgives a lot of slurs. *The Producers* is brazen—it is the very definition of chutzpah. I am reminded of my favorite moment in *Curb Your Enthusiasm*: Larry David, overheard whistling Wagner, is accused of being a self-loathing Jew.

"Jew? Yes," he responds. "Self-loathing? Yes. But self-loathing Jew? No."

Second, Brooks is an equal-opportunity offender: Jews, Jewish women, Germans, Nazis, gays, cross-dressers, Swedes—there's plenty of offense to go around.

Third, it is fair to ask: Is it really offensive?

Brooks has set *The Producers* in an idealized world that is post-World War II, but before any consciousness-raising. Bialystock and Bloom are Jews from the world of Noah's Bagels, a faraway land of nostalgic immigrant types. For Brooks, né Melvin Kaminsky in Brooklyn, it is his own Anatevka. In fact, there is a number early in the first act where all the street people, including a homeless woman, dance a hora in front of the theater to the strains of klezmer music. 'Nuff said.

Most importantly, *The Producers* is funny. Funny with the original cast, funny with the stand-in cast, funny with Jason Alexander and Martin Short.

Over the last decade, many subjects have been labeled "off-limits" for humor first by the left—the tyranny of political correctness; then by the right—not a lot laughs in our post-September 11, George W. Bush era of moral seriousness and high purpose. Over the last few decades, the Holocaust has become a subject to be confronted in classrooms, museums, monuments, movies and miniseries. In the last few weeks, *Hitler: The Rise of Evil* was a highly rated miniseries on CBS, and President Bush just visited and shed tears at Auschwitz.

The Producers is funny because it makes us laugh at things we're not supposed to laugh at. That's the transgressive part. Yes, it's a relief and it feels good to laugh at Jews, make fun of Hitler and Nazism, and leer at beautiful women who know they are sexpots—all strictly verboten. Given what we know now, of the world and of the Holocaust—and given how many Holocaust movies and documentaries we've all watched since then —the pleasures of laughing at *Springtime for Hitler* are only increased, not diminished, because there is part of us that wants to walk away from the burden of our own self-seriousness.

Brooks accomplishes that for us. In this light, Nazis goose-stepping in a Busby Berkeley-like dance number is irresistibly funny. But that's only half the equation. Transgressive alone can be funny, but also edgy and uncomfortable. The reason *The Producers* is such a success is that it is also nostalgic. It does take us back to a kinder, gentler era, to that Anatevka in Times Square, where—much like the sixties sitcom *Hogan's Heroes*—Nazis are funny. The musical numbers, too, seem to come from a familiar world—the world of musicals. No coincidence that the majority of new musicals each year are revivals (or increasingly adaptation of old films). Audiences are most comfortable with old-fashioned musicals. It should come as no surprise that Brooks straddles the old, the nostalgic and the funny with ease. He is, after all, "The 2000-year-old man."

Brooks is a genius. Geffen is a genius, too (this has nothing to do with the point I'm going to make, but it's a wise thing to say). Every so often an artist plying his trade becomes a genius. An idea comes to him or her that is so stupid—it sounds like the worst idea anyone has ever had. Imagine, for example, a comic book about the Holocaust and the difficult relationships between Holocaust survivors and their children, in which all the Jews are mice and the Nazis are cats and the mice are sent to Mauschwitz. Who could think of anything sillier? Or an Italian clown who wants to make summer camp out of a concentration camp. Stupid. Yet somehow through the strange alchemy that is art, these works, *Maus* by Art Spiegelman and *Life Is Beautiful* by Roberto Benigni, succeeded. *The Producers*, in a similar fashion, creates magic. And it's funnier.

Alexander and Short will only get better in these roles. Alexander brings an aggressive edge and Short a zaniness to what, in the end, is a love story between Bialystock and Bloom. Although I'm sure people who've never left LA County will say they could have/should have seen it in New York, the show will sell out and soon people will be coming up with any ruse to get tickets to this most entertaining of productions. I should know: For my tickets, I had to write this article.

June 6, 2003

Kitaj the 'Diasporist'

Six years have passed since painter R. B. Kitaj moved from London to Los Angeles, following a hail of criticism and counterattacks (more on that later). Recently, I visited the artist at his home and studio on the occasion of *Los Angeles Pictures*, a breathtaking exhibit at Venice's LA Louver Gallery.

Kitaj's show in Venice includes more than twenty works, paintings, drawings, even a few abstracts. Clearly, Kitaj's time in Los Angeles has been productive. But can a self-proclaimed "Diasporist" ever be truly at home?

Kitaj was born in Cleveland in 1932 and joined the merchant marines in 1949. After studying art in New York, Vienna and then London (where his classmate was David Hockney) in the 1950s, he spent the next forty years in London. In 1989, Kitaj published his polemical work, *The First Diasporist Manifesto*, which argued that the conditions of being a Jew living in the Diaspora were important elements compelling Kitaj, who was struggling to create a "Jewish art."

In 1994, the Tate Gallery in London held a retrospective of Kitaj's works, a great honor rarely accorded non-British artists. The show, which traveled to Los Angeles in 1995 (the Los Angeles County Museum of Art) and New York (the Metropolitan Museum of Art) made much of Kitaj's very distinctive use of color and figurative elements to achieve a personal iconography.

However, the English critics drew their knives and savaged the show. Schadenfreude filled the art pages.

Around the same time, Kitaj's wife, the artist Sandra Fisher, whom he married in 1983 and with whom he had a son, Max, died suddenly of a cerebral hemorrhage at age forty-seven (she was fifteen years his junior). Kitaj, in his grief, blamed her death on the bad reviews.

"No one knows what caused her hemorrhage, but stress is a contributing factor," Kitaj told me. He also blamed the bad reviews on English "low-octane anti-Semitism"—whose existence (a question of tone, a comment, a description here and there) anyone who reads the British press regularly would be hard pressed to deny.

But can anti-Semitism, no matter how low octane, explain the bad reviews? Today Kitaj refers to the episode and the accusations he made as "my Tate war."

"I fought back," he says proudly. But shortly thereafter, he moved to Los Angeles. "London also died for me," Kitaj has written.

Los Angeles holds many claims on Kitaj. His parents are buried here. His oldest daughter, Dominie, is in the Navy near San Diego (she recently served in Kuwait during the war in Iraq); his eldest son, the screenwriter Lem Dobbs, lives here with his sons in a house down the street from Kitaj, and Los Angeles is where he first met Sandra, when he was a visiting teacher at UCLA in 1970. Their son, Max, will attend college nearby next year.

Los Angeles also affected Kitaj's work in an unexpected way. "I found a strange, new romantic subject out here," Kitaj writes in the LA Louver catalogue. "Sandra and me."

Kitaj writes: "Sandra and I became lovers again, after her death, in my old age in Los Angeles, The Angels. I could make love to my angel with my paintbrush, fondle her again, caress her contours. This greatest love story ever told, the Woman-Man Story has become quite rare in painting since the death of Picasso.... I've done about twenty of these love stories so far, and our romance need not die...."

A love so great that it transcends the grave has long been the subject of art: Orpheus descended into the underworld to retrieve Eurydice but failed to bring her back. Dante went in search of his Beatrice and was able to bring her back, but he is the exception.

There is a long list of movies in which the former spouse returns, from *Blythe Spirit* to *Dona Flor* and *Ghost* (don't get me started on Demi Moore in her T-shirt. Damn you, Ashton Kutcher!). Art Buchwald even wrote a bittersweet novel, *Stella in Heaven*, in which the hero's late spouse nags him from the beyond to get a new wife.

The *Los Angeles Pictures* present Kitaj and Sandra in several guises. In one work, Kitaj clings desperately to her; in another, they meet eye to eye (though a tear drips from Kitaj's). In some, they are joined as one; in others, they are separated by a large distance.

In one painting, Kitaj suckles at her breast; in another, he grabs beneath her dress. In some, Kitaj resembles Moses, other times Freud.

In one painting, he seems angry; in others, sad, desperate. In some, Sandra's eyes are closed; in others, she looks straight ahead fiercely. She wears angel wings in some, not in others.

There are vibrant yellows and deep blues, and the canvases have more white space—all part of the way that the light and air of Los Angeles have seeped into Kitaj's work. The drawings, too, seem to have a freedom not present in his earlier work. But a question hangs over the show: What sort of love is this?

At one point, I suggested to Kitaj that the Jewish mourning process has a set form, stages and that according to Jewish tradition to mourn too much is itself a sin. Kitaj's response: "Since I don't follow all the rules, I don't follow this one either." Kitaj must do it his way.

When I visited Kitaj at his home in Los Angeles, I was led on a very proscribed guided tour—the rooms, the books, the studio—there was even a set place for us to sit and for the interview take place. He told me about his daily schedule, which is similarly regimented. Kitaj is obsessive, ritualistic, monomaniacal and his art reflects the breadth, but also the specifics, of his interests, from Aby Warburg to W. C. Fields and Weegee. Kitaj gave me some insight into what drives his critics crazy.

At the infamous Tate show, Kitaj posted text explanations next to many of the paintings, offering his own exegesis. In the reviews, the critics seemed to take particular umbrage at these passages.

For the Los Angeles show, Kitaj has offered the same key to his references, even offering the exact images that his paintings are based on. However, this time, Kitaj has left the commentary in the catalogue, rather than on the walls.

When Kitaj talks about painting in general and his paintings in specific, he talks about artists such as Giotto, Cezanne,

Matisse, Munch, etc. Some critics see it as unseemly or arrogant for Kitaj to suggest he is even in the same league as these artists.

Kitaj's work exists very much in the context of his references. It is fair to ask if an art so dependent on sources is itself original.

We are used to looking at a painting, both as viewers and critics, and having a visceral and cerebral response that determines what the work means to us. Kitaj's literal references can appear to undermine, rather than enhance that experience.

There is another way that Kitaj's work is different. Often, an artist's work can be seen as a conversation he is having with his predecessors, his contemporaries, sometimes even his critics. Kitaj's work is more one-sided.

Even as I interviewed him, it wasn't exactly a conversation. I was on the tour. My questions were anticipated, his answers were already formed. Like many an accomplished autodidact, he can no more resist being the docent of his own home than the art lecturer for his own exhibitions.

To me, the work stands on its own. However, as I struggled with what to make of Kitaj's own very specific commentaries, I seized upon Kitaj's "Jewish art." The answer was offered—no surprise—by Kitaj himself, who suggested his textual accompaniments are in the tradition of Talmudic commentaries. This begs the question: Is Kitaj the Rashi of painters?

Rabbi Joseph Telushkin in "Jewish Literacy" calls Rashi Judaism's "greatest teacher." As Telushkin explains, what so distinguished Rashi's commentaries is that when explaining the Bible or the Talmud, he wrote both about the peshat (the literal meaning) and the derash (the sermonic or allegorical meaning).

Kitaj gives us the literal by way of his references. He would like to give us the sermonic as well—but here he has a blind spot. It's his paintings themselves that are the allegory. In this department, his words carry little weight. It is our own commentaries that matter.

To the extent that Kitaj's references and commentaries overwhelm us, the work is frustrating. However, viewed on its own merit, it engages and challenges us, like a good text or even a good commentary should.

Kitaj, the Diasporist, now calls Los Angeles home. His books, his Cezannes, his Sandra surround him. So why is Los Angeles the best possible home for a Diaporist?

I think the answer can be found in a comment by the French semiotician Tsvetan Todorov, who considered California "the America of the Americas." He explained that immigrants from all over the world come to the United States, and then people from all over the states move to California. In other words, a perfect place for a Diasporist to live.

June 20, 2003

THE HEROES OF JEWISH COMEDY

On Monday, July 7, Comedy Central will premiere the first of a six-part series called *Heroes of Jewish Comedy*. Unfortunately, the series suffers for being a clip job not up to its subject. Less documentary and more comedy would help.

Produced in Britain, the show already seems dated (the series has high hopes for NBC's *The In-Laws*, a show that has already been canceled). The narration, read by iconic TV Semite Judd Hirsch, is equally underwhelming.

As my mind wandered while watching, I thought of a bleak future where the direst predictions of professional Jewish pessimists had come true: the Jewish race had disappeared, and all that was left was Holocaust memorials and Jewish museums showing this video in a hall with dioramas of Tussaud-like wax figures doing shtick. A frightening thought.

Not to worry. The true heroes of Jewish comedy in television, much like their counterparts in film, are not Jewish—at least not on screen. They remain offscreen—the writers and executives who borrowed their own personal history to create characters whose values and humor inform the American experience. This is the real assimilation—of Jewish experience and values into American culture or, as I like to call it, "the bagelization of America."

Currently the most popular sitcom on television is *Everybody Loves Raymond*. Fortunately, our home has been earthquake retrofitted, because when Raymond comes on, our house shakes, literally, with my laughter. As the credits reveal, the show is based on the comedy of Ray Romano, but the show's success owes much to executive producer Phil Rosenthal (former maitre d' at New York's PJ Bernstein Deli) and his aesthetic of pain. The Barone family may be Italian but their family psychopathology is Jewish—the vain cruel love his mother offers, the father's aggression, his brother's resentment, Ray's simultaneous embarassment, disdain and love of his parents. Rosenthal's credentials as a child of Holocaust survivors are assured (trust me on this).

Something Ain't Kosher Here: The Rise of the Jewish Sitcom by Vincent Brook details a history that begins with *The Goldbergs*, hits its apogee with *Seinfeld* and concludes that "Jewish representation on TV is no longer a big deal; it appears to be a done deal." But again, that is only if you imagine that Jewish representation is what matters.

Let's look at the history of sitcoms another way. In the beginning, working as a sitcom writer was a profession for people who were not going to be accepted in the mainstream. Jewish kids who became comics were never going to college, or were fleeing the garment industry (Carl Reiner, for example). The career path, such as it was, went: borscht belt, standup, gag writing, radio, TV. But, in class-conscious America, humor was still lower class

In the late 1960s, Doug Kenney and Henry Beard found success at the *Harvard Lampoon* creating parody magazines. Upon graduation, they saw no reason to get serious. Instead, they founded *The National Lampoon*, a magazine that captured the zeitgeist and launched the ambitions, and careers, of a generation of humorists. Only a few short years later, the pair sold out for millions. Suddenly a career in comedy became respectable.

The National Lampoon begot a radio program and then a stage show, *Lemmings*, whose cast members were recruited by Lorne Michaels for *Saturday Night Live* and were managed by Bernie Brillstein, who partnered with Brad Grey to form Brillstein-Grey Entertainment. No one would accuse Brillstein, Grey or Michaels of being part of a Jewish media cabal (at least no one we would listen to), but, like the movie moguls a century ago, their thumbprints are all over American humor. (In a similar fashion, if you look up the credits of James L. Brooks, Allan Burns and James Burrows, you get a list of almost every sitcom on TV.) But let me return to the history of employment opportunities for Harvard grads.

The next landmark occurred in the early 1990s, when Andy and Susan Borowitz created *The Fresh Prince of Bel Air*, a show about joining the mainstream in America without losing your identity. The show was based on the experiences of Benny Medina and starred the charismatic Will Smith—an African American—yet the Borowitzes, who themselves were *Harvard Lampoon* graduates, wrote a show that all Americans, but especially Jews, felt mirrored their experience "moving on up," as The Jeffersons used to say.

The Borowitzes own success made being a sitcom writer a respectable and lucrative career. For a while there it seemed as if there was a direct path from the *Lampoon* to writing on a show. It also established the precedent for a series of shows, starring charismatic African Americans (*In Living Color, Martin, The Jamie Foxx Show, Bernie Mac*) staffed by Jewish American writers. The boom years have past, but sitcom writing still remains an acceptable career ambition.

"Remember," I purr in my daughter's ear each night before she falls asleep, "funny is money."

Nonetheless, we also need to credit the executives themselves. The late Brandon Tartikoff comes to mind, but we can also look to the leadership of Colin Callender, president at HBO, and of his executive vice president of original programming, Carolyn Strauss. They stand behind the success of *The Sopranos, Sex and the City, Six Feet Under*, and *Curb Your Enthusiasm*.

In short, the heroes of Jewish comedy are not all Jewish, but in the history of the American sitcom, Jews continue to play an important—if not covert—role, fusing their sensibilities with the American mainstream. Now, that's a documentary I'd like to watch.

July 4, 2003

A Guilty Pleasure Swings with Style

Mr. S, My life with Frank Sinatra *by George Jacobs with William Stadiem*

Mr. S, My Life With Frank Sinatra by George Jacobs and William Stadiem is this summer's guilty pleasure. Jacobs was Frank Sinatra's valet from 1953 to 1968, and his memoirs are the excuse for a polished backstage tour of Sinatraland, a roller-coaster ride of the high life and the lowdown on almost every scandal, scoop, star, starlet, call girl and politician of the forties, fifties, and sixties.

I enjoy good gossip. Not the malicious betrayal of personal confidences, but the reported details of the lives of people I don't know and probably will never meet. For me, the stories of the social and the social climbers, the arrived and the arriviste, accumulate like evidence to suggest patterns about human nature. Either that or they just entertain.

I can't explain why the private dramas of people we don't know are so compelling. But the Bible is filled with them. Imagine if the tabloids covered the Good Book. I can see the headlines now: *Eve—Her Bite With the Serpent! Abraham and Sara: Their Struggle to Have a Child! Breaking News: Accused Cain's Plaintive Plea: "Am I My Brother's Keeper?"* Time moves on, but we remain human. As Philip Roth suggested in *The Human Stain*, perhaps a banner should have been hung across the Clinton White House proclaiming: "A HUMAN BEING LIVES HERE."

Cafe society has often inspired literature: Thackeray, Proust, Zola were all chroniclers of, as Balzac put it, "harlots high and low." In our own time, newspaper gossip columns from Winchell to Rush & Molloy, have provided a running commentary on the demimonde as successive generations fade in and out of bold print. It's not Howard Zinn's *People's History*; more like the *People* magazine history of "hanging out." So let me be clear—lest you had any doubts—*Mr. S* is not literature, but it is a fun read; an enjoyable dose of high-quality gossip.

George Jacobs, New Orleans born, black and Jewish (Sinatra got him interested in his religion, took him to Israel and arranged for his late-in-life bar mitzvah), was the outsider in the ultimate insider's world. He found a kindred spirit in Bill Stadiem, in part because of Bill's own outsider status, having grown up Southern and Jewish in North Carolina.

Stadiem is a friend of mine. We first met in a far-away galaxy called the 1980s. Stadiem was held up to me as someone who had achieved the remarkable: A Harvard Law grad, he had recently left Sullivan & Cromwell, the prestigious white-shoe Wall Street firm, and then wrote two books, *A Class by Themselves*, a serious volume on the Southern Aristocracy, and *Marilyn Monroe Confidential* a racy tome by Lena Pepitone, Marilyn Monroe's maid.

Over the years, Stadiem continued to bounce between serious volumes, such as *Too Rich*, a fascinating bio of Egypt's King Farouk, and *Madame 90210*, the memoirs of Beverly Hills' infamous Madame Alex. Stadiem has done it all, freelancing for every magazine here and in Europe, and selling the occasional screenplay (Stadiem wrote *Young Toscanini*, a Zeffirelli film that became a Liz Taylor fiasco).

One day attorney Henry Bushkin (as Johnny Carson used to call him) asked Stadiem to lunch at Matteo's, the old-guard establishment in Westwood, to introduce him to Jacobs—who lives in Palm Springs as a master carpenter, and who was considering telling his story. I have joked that Stadiem should open a domestic agency so he can place future sources, but in George Jacobs, Stadiem found what he called, "a live one."

As a result, *Mr. S* swings with style, filled with ring-a-ding-ding detail. Stadiem has poured a lifetime of accumulated gossip into every chapter. Stars, politicians, potentates, pimps, hookers, drug dealers—Stadiem knows these characters and as Jacobs brings them into the narrative, they are painted with verisimilitude. As the anecdotes accumulate—and many of the stories are too salacious to repeat here—you get a sense of the characters of Sinatra, Ava Gardner, Marilyn Monroe, Dean Martin, Sammy Davis, Jr., and the influences and events that propelled them onto the public imagination.

Unfortunately, the book turns sour at the end, and Sinatra, who early on is a complex but genuine character, morphs into a cruel, empty and unredeemed persona. Apparently, Hell hath no fury like a domestic dispatched.

Reading *Mr. S* it might be fair to ask, as reviewers have, how it is that George Jacobs—whose service to the Chairman of the

Board ended in 1968—could possibly recall so many details. Good question. It helps that most of the tarnished are no longer among the living.

For *Mr. S*, as with most gossip columns, truth itself is, as fabulist Jerzy Kosinski once wrote, "a temporary resolution of various contradictions." And a guilty pleasure of summer.

July 18, 2003

THE GENIUS OF *THE PRODUCERS*

To understand something of the success of *The Producers,* it helps to understand something of its history. There is probably no person on the planet who doesn't know the story of how this sensation of a musical came to pass, but let me quickly recap:

In the early sixties, Mel Brooks writes the book for the Charles Strouse-Lee Adams musical, *All American.* Their last musical, *Bye Bye Birdie,* was a hit. *All American* was not. Brooks wonders: What if it was intentional? From that germ of an idea, and a character Brooks worked for briefly after World War II, came the movie, *The Producers.*

This movie about a flop that becomes a hit followed a similar trajectory. The studio was so convinced the film was unmarketable, that it sat on the shelf, the story goes, until Peter Sellers screened it and called it the funniest movie he'd ever seen.

The movie was released, and Brooks won an Oscar for the screenplay. That was in 1968. More than thirty years later, Brooks gets a call from David Geffen who insists it become a musical. Brooks tries to say no, but who says no to Geffen? Thank God Geffen didn't call about *Spaceballs.*

In the end, so many producers came aboard that Geffen stepped aside. Sometimes being smarter than everyone else is reward enough.

The overwhelmingly talented Susan Stroman joined the creative team as director-choreographer; William Ivey Long did the costumes; Robin Wagner the sets. Brooks (with Thomas Meehan) wrote the book, and Brooks wrote more than twenty songs. The show was a smash, and the rest is Tony history.

The irony is that by the turn of the millennium, Brooks had pretty much worn out his welcome in Hollywood. He had not had a hit in years, his humor seemed too old-fashioned and shticky and he had a maddening habit of inserting musical production numbers into his movies at a time when no one was interested in musicals. Go figure.

In spite of all this—and, at the same time, because of all this—*The Producers* became a success. The staging, the sets, the costumes, the choreography, the supporting roles, the showgirls—all great. The conceit of the show within a show, the flop that becomes a hit, became a hit. But that is not the main reason for its success: The whole production works, because it is at the same time nostalgic and transgressive (transgressive is a word that I have always wanted to use in order to garner the attention and respect of academics. I'm not exactly sure what it means, but I will tell you what I am referring to).

Brooks has created characters to bring tears of joy to any anti-Semite. The heroes, so called, are Max Bialystock, a theatrical producer who swindles old ladies out of their savings by seducing them (a cheat and a gigolo!), and Leo Bloom, a nebbish accountant who abandons his morals for the casting couch and finds his shiksa goddess in the ululating secretary-actress Ulla.

Not to sound like Julius Streicher (or the punch line of one of my favorite jokes) but one could ask: What is it about you people and money? Yet I would venture to guess very few complaints have been lodged at the Anti-Defamation League and the Simon Wiesenthal Center.

There are many possible explanations. First and foremost, Brooks' exuberance in both being Jewish and making fun of Jews forgives a lot of slurs. *The Producers* is brazen—it is the very definition of chutzpah. I am reminded of my favorite moment in *Curb Your Enthusiasm:* Larry David, overheard whistling Wagner, is accused of being a self-loathing Jew.

"Jew? Yes," he responds. "Self-loathing? Yes. But self-loathing Jew? No."

Second, Brooks is an equal-opportunity offender: Jews, Jewish women, Germans, Nazis, gays, cross-dressers, Swedes—there's plenty of offense to go around.

Third, it is fair to ask: Is it really offensive?

Brooks has set *The Producers* in an idealized world that is post-World War II, but before any consciousness-raising. Bialystock and Bloom are Jews from the world of Noah's Bagels, a faraway land of nostalgic immigrant types.

For Brooks, nee Melvin Kaminsky in Brooklyn, it is his own Anatevka. In fact, there is a number early in the first act where all the street people, including a homeless woman, dance a hora in front of the theater to the strains of klezmer music. 'Nuff said.

Most importantly, *The Producers* is funny. Funny with the original cast; funny with the stand-in cast. It opens at the Orange County Performing Arts Center this week, starring Bob Amaral as Bialystock and Andy Taylor as Bloom.

Over the last decade, many subjects have been labeled "off-limits" for humor, first by the left—the tyranny of political correctness; then by the right—not a lot laughs in our post-September 11, George W. Bush-era of moral seriousness and high purpose. Over the last few decades, the Holocaust has become a subject to be confronted in classrooms, museums, monuments, movies and miniseries. Last season, *Hitler: The Rise of Evil* was a highly rated miniseries on CBS, and Bush visited and shed tears at Auschwitz.

The Producers is funny because it makes us laugh at things we're not supposed to laugh at. That's the transgressive part. Yes, it's a relief, and it feels good to laugh at Jews, make fun of Hitler and Nazism and leer at beautiful women who know they are sexpots—all strictly verboten.

Given what we know now of the world and of the Holocaust -- and given how many Holocaust movies and documentaries we've all watched since then—the pleasures of laughing at "Springtime for Hitler" are only increased, not diminished, because there is part of us that wants to walk away from the burden of our own self-seriousness.

Brooks accomplishes that for us. In this light, Nazis goose-stepping in a Busby Berkeley-like dance number is irresistibly funny. But that's only half the equation. Transgressive alone can be funny, but also edgy and uncomfortable.

The reason *The Producers* is such a success is that it is also nostalgic. It does take us back to a kinder, gentler era, to that Anatevka in Times Square, wheres—much like the sixties sitcom, *Hogan's Heroes*—Nazis are funny.

The musical numbers, too, seem to come from a familiar world—the world of musicals. No coincidence that the majority of new musicals each year are revivals (or increasingly adaptation of old films). Audiences are most comfortable with old-fashioned musicals.

It should come as no surprise that Brooks straddles the old, the nostalgic and the funny with ease. He is, after all, "The 2000-year-old man."

Brooks is a genius. Geffen is a genius, too (this has nothing to do with the point I'm going to make, but it's a wise thing to say). Every so often, an artist plying his trade becomes a genius. An idea comes to him or her that is so stupid—it sounds like the worst idea anyone has ever had.

Imagine, for example, a comic book about the Holocaust and the difficult relationships between Holocaust survivors and their children, in which all the Jews are mice and the Nazis are cats, and the mice are sent to Mauschwitz. Who could think of anything sillier? Or an Italian clown who wants to make summer camp out of a concentration camp. Stupid.

Yet somehow through the strange alchemy that is art, these works, "Maus," by Art Spiegelman, and "Life Is Beautiful," by Roberto Benigni, succeeded. *The Producers,* in a similar fashion, creates magic. And it's funnier.

August 5, 2005

Maahj Cracks Fashionistas

The Maah-jong craze

What, you may be asking yourself, is the next hot trend? The style universe looks to Los Angeles in general, and this column in particular, for those cutting-edge trends that define the culture. No wonder this column has become such a favorite of trendsetters and fashionistas everywhere. (Nonetheless, I continue to deny "sexing up" reports for W, Ingrid Sischy, Kal Ruttenstein, Bonnie Fuller or Hello! Magazine—no matter what the BBC claims.)

But back to the future: A movement is happening. LA women—for whom kabbalah is so two years ago—who've been wearing Havaiana flip-flops since way before last summer, are meeting all over town. They're finished with health clubs, they're beyond personal trainers. They may have their own yoga mats, but they've long abandoned Yoga Works, Bikram and Maha Yoga and moved on to a smaller studio you haven't heard of—yet. They no longer care about Manolos, think Jimmy Choos are for *Sex and the City* clones and Sigerson Morrison was yesterday. They're over with Burberry's plaids. No. No. No. So what are the relentlessly trendy up to?

What they are doing is playing mahjongg. That's right. The American version of the ancient Chinese tile game once played by old ladies in Miami Beach is now the passion of the beyond-fashion-forward women in Los Angeles. I refer, of course, to my wife and her friends. Listen closely, and you'll hear the click clack of tiles and hands moving around the table.

I date the current mahjongg explosion to the moment when Jill Nadlman's monthly all-women poker game decided to learn "maahj," as they call it. They're in so deep they started a separate maahj evening. Word got around. Suddenly maahj is everywhere.

There's a game happening over breakfast at the Kinara Spa and Cafe on Robertson Boulevard. Someone's got a room at the Bel Air Hotel for afternoon games. Last week, there was a lunch at a private home in Beverly Hills. You won't be surprised to hear that a group of übermoms from the Center for Early Education have a group. Or that the A-list at Brentwood needed to have their own. It is spreading—fast.

Which is why I am sitting in Johnni Levene's home in Rustic Canyon. Levene collects and deals in antique mahjongg sets. She has offered to show me her collection and give me a little tutorial in the "chirping sparrows" (mahjongg).

Mahjongg for the uninitiated, is a Chinese game with beginnings some attribute to Confucius himself. It was introduced to the English clubs in Shanghai in the early 1900s by two brothers named White. In 1920, Standard Oil's man in Soochow, Joseph Babcock, came up with a standardized set of rules for Americans. By 1923, the craze was so big that sales of mahjongg sets topped 1.5 million dollars in the United States.

Levene is an obsessive collector—her prior obsessions have included vintage aquarium mermaids (made in Japan in the 1950s), Victorian butterfly jewelry and Enid Collins purses. Five years ago, she spotted her first mahjongg set at a flea market. What she saw delighted and horrified her. She loved the artistry of the hand carved tiles, but someone had drilled holes in them to make them into bracelets. Levene now had a mission: She would rescue mahjongg sets from the drillers. Several hundred sets later, she is making headway.

The Chinese game was played with 144 tiles, the American is now played with 152 (144 plus eight jokers). Herein lies where collectors go crazy: some sets are incomplete. In some, the tiles have aged poorly. Levene lists the main criteria as: condition, color, artistry and rarity. What Levene does is restore and complete the sets, sometimes restoring not only the tiles, but the cradles they sit in and the cases that hold them. Like all things worth collecting, each can be a work of art.

There are more than 300 sets in Levene's mahjongg room. Although sets have been made in bone, celluloid, ivory (mostly traveling sets) and modern plastics, Levene's favorites are the bakelite/catalin sets, which were discontinued in the 1960s. Levene's vintage sets run anywhere from 100 dollars to 950 dollars. In her own collection, the holy grail is "enrobed" sets that feature two colors, one encircling the other.

Why mahjongg now? Levene suggest two reasons. First, after September 11, more people wanted to stay in or entertain privately, and second, as she says, "It's hard for girls to find something to do together." (Better she says it than me.)

Levene is on to something: in Los Angeles a Chinese/Jewish tile game, played by our ancestors, creates bonds between women and history that no spiritual or athelitic trend can.

Personally, I was hoping the whole "pole dancing as exercise" fad was going to catch on. But fashion serves a fickle master. Right now the craze is for maahj. In Los Angeles, as Don Henley's buddy, Thoreau, once said: "We worship not the Graces, nor the Parcae, but Fashion."

August 15, 2003

Romancing the Industry

Matchmaker Samantha Daniels

Los Angeles is often depicted as a hedonist's pleasure palace adorned with beauty and perfumed by sex. But where, oh where, is the romance? In a city devoted to storytelling, how do you find the fairy-tale happy ending and meet the person you will marry?

I arrived in Los Angeles already one of the "smug marrieds," as Bridget Jones might say. By now I am more married, less smug. I keep a straight eye on the coupling pursuits of my friends who wonder how they went from single to unmarried. They ask, as Vladimir Ilych once wrote: "What Is to Be Done?"

Samantha Daniels, the self-proclaimed "headhunter of love," says she can help.

You know that impulse to fix people up? Daniels has not only turned that impulse into her business, Samantha's Table, but also into a Darren Star-created TV program, *Miss Match,* premiering on NBC this fall starring Alicia Silverstone. Everything old is new again.

Samantha is very much the 21st-century matchmaker. She sees herself in Hollywood terms as a "talent agent." Banish all thoughts of Lainie Kazan. No cliché frumpy, meddling yenta is she. Instead, she's an engaging, well-put-together professional in her early thirties. For someone who has a personal trainer, a therapist, a life coach, an agent and/or a business manager, why not a dating coach?

A graduate of Penn and Temple Law, Daniels was a matrimonial (divorce) attorney practicing in New York and then in Philadelphia with her father before launching her career as a matchmaker three and a half years ago. She decided bringing people together was a happier enterprise than presiding at the dissolution.

Her first fix up was in college between her roommate and a friend from high school. It succeeded. She then began throwing parties and events for singles. She realized that she had a near-photographic memory for faces and details and started organizing her information on a computer. She now has a database of several thousand singles that she consults. Earlier this year, Daniels brought her business to Los Angeles.

Here's how it works: An initial sixty- to ninety-minute consultation at Samantha's Table runs $400, and clients have to fill out a detailed questionnaire.

"I spend time talking to people," Daniels says. "They tell me their 'preferences' and their 'deal-breakers.'"

She then sets them up with people who fall in between. She does not buy the adage "opposites attract."

"Relationships are hard enough," she says.

Daniels only engages those clients she likes. And, of course, they must like her. She is like a friend. However, no matter how excited she gets about bringing the right couple together, matchmaking is still—for her—a business. After the consultation, the client selects a package of dates and services. The prices vary.

As she says, “Some people know what they are looking for; others figure it out along the way.”

She has a full list of complementary services, including a stylist, a concierge and even a psychic.

Daniels works one-on-one. She sets up the first date, where it is always drinks and the guy always pays. Those are her rules. Daniels will even coach you on Internet dating (her opinion on it is: be careful, but whatever gets you more options is worth pursuing). Her clientele is both male and female, Jewish and non-Jewish. She has not done a gay fix-up—yet. But she does have thirty-nine marriages to her credit so far, and many more in serious relationships.

Some common dating mistakes?

“Some women dress too provocatively. At the same time, some men are too sloppy.”

Daniels fine tunes her clients. She says one of the biggest obstacles to finding true love is giving up too soon.

“Everyone has a story—everyone has an interesting life,” she says.

Most happy couples, she points out, did not find love at first sight, it took a couple of dates to sink in (at least that’s what my wife tells me).

Most important: “You have to be ready and you have to meet someone who is ready,” she says.

So what has she observed about daters in Los Angeles?

“In LA there’s a disconnect: The women think the men are not interested in someone like them,” Daniels says. “They assume they only want to date MAWs [model/actress/whatever].

The men, for their part, complain they can't meet anyone 'real.' They assume the women are only interested in their wallets, their cars, their jobs. But actually, they are both looking for the same thing: someone to love."

Her bottom line: "You don't need to find 1,000 right people. Just one."

Daniels is more the traditional Jewish matchmaker than she lets on. She believes that people are meant to be couples.

"Noah's Ark was two by two," she says.

Yet she is single. She confesses that she was too focused on her career.

"Now," she says, "I'm ready."

Is Los Angeles ready? I think so. Not just for Daniels. The time has come for Los Angeles to go from sex to romance.

August 28, 2003

Einstein in California

One hundred years ago, Einstein was a Zurich Polytechnic teaching graduate who couldn't land a job in academe. Instead, he got a position as a patent clerk in Bern, Switzerland. Not the most challenging job, but it gave him time to think.

Einstein liked to conduct what he called "thought experiments," one of which asked: "What would a beam of light look like if you could race besides it?"

During the course of 1905, what has come to be called Einstein's "miracle year," he published four scientific papers, including his paper on "special relativity," which answered the question posed above. The answer is easier understood today if you replace the beam of light with a car. From the sidewalk, the car looks like it's speeding by. But if you drive alongside the car, it doesn't seem to be moving. By demonstrating the relativity of time and space, Einstein unshackled the perception that they were absolutes.

Within a decade, Joyce wrote *Ulysses*, a chronicle of a single day rendered with stream of consciousness; Proust was working on his own meditation on space and time, *Remembrance of Things Past*; Picasso painted *Les Demoiselles D'Avignon* and made his first abstract sculptures; Nijinsky danced to Stravinsky's *Rites of Spring*; while in Vienna, Freud was conducting his own thought experiments, charting a psychic interior world as unexplored as space itself.

A coincidence? Or a reaction to the industrialization of society? Either way, the reaction to the zeitgeist of relativity in science and culture was quickly followed by World War I and the Russian Revolution. Einstein began his search for a unifying principle of physics, perhaps in order to envision a universe where opposites would co-exist rather than clash.

Einstein made three visits to California in the early 1930s, working at Caltech in Pasadena. As described in *A Lone Traveler: Einstein in California* by Rabbi William Kramer with Margaret Leslie Davis, which the Skirball is publishing in connection with its "Einstein" exhibit, Einstein received the star treatment: Studio owner Carl Laemmle led Einstein on the Universal tour and invited him to a screening of the anti-war classic *All Quiet on the Western Front.* Jack Warner (one of the original Warner brothers) told him, "You know, I have a theory about relatives, too—don't hire them."

Einstein met all Hollywood's then-reigning stars as well as Los Angeles' Jewish elite. He dined at Pickfair with America's sweetheart Mary Pickford and her husband Douglas Fairbanks. He ate on several occasions at Charlie Chaplin's and was his guest at the premiere of *City Lights*, where Einstein's fame seemed to eclipse Chaplin's. He attended services and played violin at Temple B'nai Israel in Pasadena. He conferred with Wilshire Boulevard Temple's Rabbi Edgar Magnin. He spoke at Jewish fundraisers supporting a Zionist homeland and the creation of Hebrew University in Jerusalem.

It would be easy to argue that these visits were insignificant, but in fact California was a turning point in Einstein's life—in many ways it shaped the second part of his life.

The Skirball is offering a special interactive exhibit on Einstein in California, "Three Winters in the Sun," created by USC/Annenberg's Labyrinth Project. Not part of the New York Museum of Natural History show, the installation focuses on six compartments of Einstein's world: his own household, science, émigrés, Jews, Hollywood and the FBI, which began a file on Einstein that eventually reached 1,400 pages.

Labyrinth Project Director Marsha Kinder, a professor of critical studies at USC, believes Einstein's time in California was "transformative."

For example, consider Einstein's friendship with Chaplin. Einstein found in Chaplin and his "Little Tramp" a simpatico spirit. Erik Erikson and Roman Jakobson have written about Einstein's use of nonverbal language: Einstein's great salve was music; his most eloquent expression was in mathematics. Chaplin was also a master of nonverbal communication. Even after sound was introduced, Chaplin's tramp remained silent.

Einstein learned of fame from Chaplin. When Einstein asked Chaplin under the glare of klieg lights what it all meant, Chaplin replied, "Nothing, absolutely nothing." But Einstein knew better. He used his celebrity to speak out for pacifism, for Zionism and against the Nazis.

Perhaps Einstein had some impact on Chaplin as well: When Chaplin bade farewell to the tramp, his first sound comedy was the anti-Hitler, anti-fascist satire *The Great Dictator.*

By the end of Einstein's third sojourn in California, Germany had come under the force of its own unifying theory: National Socialism. Einstein realized that he would have to give up his home and live as an émigré in America. Einstein also accepted that his celebrity imposed a responsibility and a duty to speak out. As Kinder pointed out in a recent conversation, as the most famous living Jew at the time, Einstein was living denial of Hitler's claims of inferiority.

Anti-Semitism made Einstein a Jew and an even more ardent Zionist. Einstein's God, like his science, was a unifier, not a divider—and if his mathematical formulas tried to explain how planets and atoms should behave, his religion attempted to do the same for people.

As Einstein said at a 1931 Jewish National Fund dinner held at the Ambassador Hotel in Los Angeles: "Out of our community of interests there has at all times risen men who have embodied the conscience of the western world, men who were defenders of humanity and justice."

George Dyson, the science historian, wondered in the Einstein issue of Discover magazine, "What if Einstein had stayed at Caltech?" Expounding on his "What if?" Dyson told me "We will never know… But what if he surfed?" Would Einstein, living in California, among the stars in heaven and on earth, have figured out the ultimate fate of the universe?

We have crossed from the 20th to the 21st century on a wave of technological and scientific innovation. Yet, as we become increasingly interconnected in a rush of globalization, our current modernity has provoked another outbreak of war, extremism and anti-Semitism.

Einstein is back in California, at the Skirball until May 2005. More than ever, Dr. Einstein, we need a theory that will reconcile that which polarizes us.

September 2, 2004

Summer Reading

Sandor Marai's Embers, *Gunter Grass'* The Crab

I had planned to spend my summer in Hollywood. I had teed up on my reading list *Maneater* by Gigi Levangie Grazer, *Action!* by Robert Cort and *San Remo Drive* by Leslie Epstein. But, as Primo Levi used to say, life proved otherwise.

I had high hopes for *Maneater*. I like Grazier's scripts and, as the wife of producer Brian Grazer, she is uniquely poised to see and hear a lot of dish. However, the accumulation of sordid details overwhelmed me. It was like being at an extravagant buffet where you keep tasting to find the best bits but end the evening with a stomachache. It put me off my reading plan. It turns out that one swallow of *Maneater* does a summer make.

Instead, I found myself one evening at Villa Aurora, a mansion in the Pacific Palisades. In the 1940s, German novelist Lion Feuchtwanger lived there, and his home became a salon for émigré intellectuals. Today it is home to a foundation devoted to bringing European intellectuals to Los Angeles.

I was the guest of the Getty Museum's own resident European intellectual and newly minted noble, Sir Kenneth ("Just call me Ken") Robinson. Ken, the Getty's education Guru, is very funny and very charming, but the evening, devoted to translation, was painfully boring. So much so that we both fled and consoled ourselves with burgers at Father's Office—so the evening wasn't a total loss. Also we did manage a quick tour of Feuchtwanger's private library. The names on the bindings—Stefan Sweig, Herman Broch, Arthur Schnitzler — belonged to another era. But they reminded me that not every novel need explain (and feel like) a Brazilian bikini wax.

So I found myself returning to Central Europe for my summer reading. I had not been there in a long, long time. Once upon a time, in a galaxy far away called high school, I got hooked on German novels. I read all of Hermann Hesse, from *Siddhartha* (very high school hippie), to the dark *Steppenwolf* and ending up at the esoteric *The Glass Bead Game.* It was only a short few years later that I was scaling that literary Everest, Thomas Mann's *The Magic Mountain.* I got so in so deep I developed a psychosomatic fever. Soon after I left the Germans for the Russians. Goodbye Hans Castorp, hello Prince Mishkin! As I said, it was a long time ago.

So this summer, whether by chance or intent, the three best novels I read were all from the other side of the Atlantic, all from Mitteleuropa: *Crabwalk* by Gunter Grass, *Embers* by Sandor Marai, and *Azarel* by Karoly Pap.

Embers might well be the best novel I've read this year. Little happens—yet the novel is about all that is important in life. An old man living in an ancestral castle deep in the Carpathian forest receives a dinner visit from the best friend of his youth, who left his home without explanation forty-one years ago—after which the old general never spoke to his wife again. Was there a betrayal? Will a duel ensue? Will all be explained? That is what keeps you turning the pages. (Fellow producers, hold on: It's already been optioned and will star Sean Connery and Winona Ryder.) Marai was born in Hungary in 1900, but arrived in the United States after the Holocaust. He lived for many years in San Diego where he died in 1989—a suicide.

Crabwalk explores German guilt in three successive generations surrounding the sinking of a German ship, the Wilhelm Gustloff, by the Russians, a true event with a greater civilian toll than the sinking of the Titanic. Nobel prize-winning Grass' deftness as a novelist allows him to "crabwalk" sideways in time and plot to discuss the Holocaust, neo-Nazi revisionists, Stalin and German reunification. It is a masterful work that raises important questions while providing a gripping drama that surprises to the end.

Finally, *Azarel* is a lost classic recently translated and published in English by Steerforth Press. Originally published in Budapest in 1937, *Azarel* tells the story of a young child who not only rebels against his family—modern Orthodox Hungarian Jews—but also against God. At the time, *Azarel* was regarded as controversial for several reasons: Literary writers, even those who were Jewish, never wrote about Jewish matters. Pap did so, but in a Hungarian understandable to Jew and non-Jew alike. Second, he didn't write about Jews in Hungarian society, rather he revealed the inner dramas of the observant community. Finally, he cast a critical eye on the believers and the hypocrisy of those who observed but didn't believe. Pap ominously predicted that Hungarian Jews would disappear in a pyre of their own making. This did not endear him to the Hungarian Jewish community.

In 1944, Pap was arrested for being a Jew and sent to Buchenwald. There, his fellow inmates offered to smuggle him out so he could write about the camp. He refused. In 1945 he was transferred to Bergen-Belsen where he died.

Azarel is a tough read. The sentences are terse, the writing dense. Pages do not fly by. I had to take a break halfway in. But it is the intensity of Pap's emotion and his powers of observation that make *Azarel* a literary masterwork that feels contemporary—as if Daphne Merkin and Allegra Goodman had rewritten Harold Brodkey.

My summer in Mitteleuropa was, to quote The Grateful Dead, "a long strange trip." But like all good vacations, my summer reading took me to places I'd never been, taught me things I never knew and gave me pleasures I never expected. All that without ever leaving home.

September 12, 2003

Budapest in LA

In the coming weeks I will spend many dreamy hours inside Wilshire Boulevard Temple. Two blocks east of Western on Wilshire, the landmark building is an imposing and awe-inspiring architectural gem that belongs to that school of temple architecture that says: We Jews are citizens, and our house of worship is as glorious as any non-Jewish one—maybe more so.

Wilshire Boulevard Temple was completed in 1929, the same year as New York's Temple Emanu-El, the world's largest synagogue. The world's second-largest synagogue is the Dohany Utca Synagogue in Budapest, Hungary, dedicated in 1859. I was in Budapest last week and spent time in the synagogue thinking about my own family's deep connection to the city, wondering whether Los Angeles will be the Budapest of the 21st century.

One hundred years ago, Budapest was home to the wealthiest, most educated, most assimilated Jewish society since—to paraphrase JFK—Moses Maimonides dined alone. Hungarian Jews essentially formed the middle and upper class of Hungarian society, dominating business, science, arts and letters. They even had their own liberal variant of Judaism called "Neolog" of which the Dohany was its temple.

My connections to Budapest and to the Dohany synagogue run deep. My great-grandfather, Bela Hatschek, was married in the Dohany Temple, on July 4, 1886. His mother-in-law, Jeannette Reizer Back, attended the wedding and her grave marker still stands in the Salgotarjani Utca cemetery which I visited last week. Bela Hatschek owned Budapest's first car, a 1894 Benz Velo which he brought in from Germany on a flatbed train in 1896. His daughter Adrienne (my grandmother) married Kornel Saar. She was a stage actress who performed at Budapest's Opera House. Kornel Saar, my grandfather, was related to Theodore Herzl, who lived in the building next to the Dohany Temple and which now houses the Jewish Museum.

As a young girl my mother attended the Dohany Temple, looking out from the balcony to check out the young men downstairs. She too was an actress, and she performed small roles in films, including one I watched recently written by Erno Szep who would later write the Holocaust memoir, *The Smell of Humans.*

My father was born in Poland but spent part of the war years in Budapest. In 1988, a Holocaust memorial was dedicated in the courtyard of the Dohany Synagogue. I attended with my parents, at which time my father was given an award in the Dohany Utca Synagogue for his work on behalf of Hungarian Jewry. My father died 10 years ago. Since then a plaque was placed on the memorial in his honor, which I got to see for the first time last week. It reads "Bruce B. Teicholz, a leader of the Jewish Resistance, 1942-1945, he will be remembered for the lives he saved."

At one time, one-third of all Budapest's residents were Jewish. By the 1930s, many Hungarian Jews had changed their German-sounding names to Hungarian ones.

There are those who would see in the assimilation of Hungarian Jewry a morality tale, with the Nazis and the Holocaust being the price one pays. But the reality is that the Nazis were nondenominational in their anti-Semitism, murdering Chasids alongside converts to Christianity. The lesson, if there is one, is that assimilation affords no protection from anti-Semitism. But that does not mean that the success of Budapest's Jewish community cannot inspire us today in Los Angeles.

When the first National Jewish Population Survey was published a decade ago, pundits and proselytizers argued that the only way to stem the loss of Jewish identity was to combat the dual sins of assimilation and intermarriage. Suddenly, Jewish day schools were opening as fast as coffee joints. Now a new survey has been published, and it once again begs the question: What is the best way to cultivate a vibrant Jewish population?

I say we focus on the majority of Jews who view their Judaism as one item on a list of characteristics that begins with American. Let us celebrate Jewish values, Jewish culture, Jewish achievement. Let us not be afraid to have Judaism be a part of who we are, but also a part of being American. Let us make Los Angeles the Budapest of the 21st century, a place where Judaism is part and parcel of the city's cultural landscape.

Southern California influences TV, movies, fashion, sports, and science.

Los Angeles is where the world's Jewish communities are migrating. We have one of the oldest exile communities, the Persian Jews, right here. The European exiles of the 1930s as well as plenty of New Yorkers and a healthy dose of Israelis and citizens from the former Soviet Republics travel down the same freeways. All are potent ingredients for a 21st Century goulash that speaks of our strengths as a people and as a community. That's food for thought — or at least what I'll be thinking about as I gaze upon the gorgeous murals inside the Wilshire Boulevard Temple.

September 26, 2003

A Reality of Their Own

Reality TV Producers

Reality TV is nothing new. Since the dawn of television, there have always been unscripted formats and game shows of one kind or another. However, the current incarnation of reality programming—shows such as *Survivor*, *The Bachelor*, and *Fear Factor*—may be the most durable and successful shows in the history of reality programming. What's more, reality TV is the most innovative area of current programming, far more creative than sitcoms, hour-long dramas, sports, news or movies and miniseries. In fact, it may be helpful to think of current reality shows as game shows or "event programming" much like the highly touted TV movies of the 1970s and '80s.

I learned all this and more when I attended a recent panel at The Museum of Television and Radio in Beverly Hills called, "Keeping it Real: The Past, Present and Future of Reality Television."

Hosted by the museum's vice president and director Barbara Dixon, the panelists included the producers and executives most responsible for the current craze, including Mike Darnell,

Fox's reality guru; Mike Fleiss, the executive producer of the highly addictive *The Bachelor* and *The Bachelorette*; Ghen Maynard, the CBS executive behind *Survivor*; Jonathan Murray of Bunim-Murray's *The Real World* and *Road Rules*; Arnold Shapiro, who produces *Big Brother*; Scott Stone, of Stone Stanley Productions, who produced *Celebrity Mole* and *Fame*; and Andrea Wong, ABC's reality exec.

Dixon led the panel in a discussion of their programs' antecedents and influences: the 1973 PBS documentary, *An American Family*; raw reality shows like *COPS* and *Rescue 911*, which Shapiro produced; and MTV's *The Real World*. I am happy to tell you that neither Dickens nor Shakespeare was cited, but these are intelligent people who know exactly what they are doing.

What I learned was this: When all is said and done, a reality show is about inexpensive, compelling TV programming. Like scripted shows, reality programs are driven by story and character, and sold on an explosive idea that you can promote in thirty seconds. Casting is critical—it's part of how the producers influence story. The audiences are, for the most part, women ages eighteen to thirty-four. Although there is no script, there is editing and music and the host to help shape a final product.

You may think that anything goes, but the producers are keenly conscious of the shifting lines they will not cross. As one panelist put it bluntly, "No one wants to have the first show that someone dies on." But one thing is clear: the producers and executives are following their gut instincts to guess what it is America wants.

Darnell, the executive who was reality TV before reality TV was cool (remember *When Animals Attack*?) described the current shows as "social psychology experiments." Darnell is right, perhaps more than he knows.

One hundred years ago, as Neal Gabler so ably chronicled in *An Empire of Their Own*, a group of mostly Jewish immigrants and their children settled in California and founded a movie industry that defined the American dream from their own inner strivings, dreams and projections.

Today, television reaches far more Americans than movies. More hours of television programming are devoted to reality than to news. I would argue that it is no coincidence that these are the producers and executives defining our reality.

Looking out at the panel—what you did not see was prototypical all-Americans, Mayflower descendants or the prom king and queen. They are, as a group, the outsiders.

Fleiss says he turned to reality TV because he was a failed sitcom writer. Wang started in strategic planning; Maynard in drama. Darnell has endured a lifetime of mocking on his road to success.

For the first generation of movie moguls it was enough to present America as they imagined it. But for these executives and producers, born in America, living in California, the children and grandchildren of immigrants (literally or figuratively), they have looked inward to create programming based on their own neurotic reactions to the American dream.

What are *Survivor*, *Fear Factor*, *Big Brother*, *Joe Millionaire* and *American Idol* if not the inner drama of the outsider wanting to conquer the American mainstream? Each show is like the deepest anxiety of any teenager: Will I be tough enough? Am I a wimp? Is everyone watching me? Do people like me for me? And increasingly, there is another question in America: Can I be famous?

Consider these programs: twenty-five women vie for the attention of one bachelor; twenty-five men vie for the affections of one dream woman. Are these our dreams, or the revenge fantasy of the outcast? And just who considers their children such princes or princesses? How about this show: Parents choose the right partner for their child, resorting to a lie-detector test at one point. Whose parents interfere too much in their child's selection of a mate? Just ask Nia Vardalos, who made a fortune off her *Big Fat Greek Wedding*. She knows.

If you asked these producers and executives about their inspiration, they would say one thing: they create shows that first, they believe they can sell, and second, shows whose concepts grab them. It is a subjective call—and that's the point—their own sensibilities are informing America's reality. One-hundred years after the moguls ruled Hollywood, a new generation has plumbed its own dreams and neuroses to create a reality of its own.

October 10, 2003

Making LA Real

Developer Larry Fields and architect Frank Gehry

This weekend the story of Los Angeles, and its future, is all about one building, the Walt Disney Concert Hall. Critics have already hailed our new symphony hall as a triumph of design, determination and a marriage of form, function and acoustic feng shui. But more significantly, in the Walt Disney Concert Hall, Los Angeles is finally acknowledging Frank Gehry's central role in our culture. One building, as Gehry taught us with Bilbao, can change a city (even as the destruction of buildings, such as the World Trade Center, can change not only a city, but a nation—even the world).

Real estate touches our lives so pervasively that sometimes we take its impact for granted. The buildings we live in, the ones in which we work, what we see as we make our daily rounds—their shape, the materials they are made of, their density, how we interact with them and the light and air—all aggregate to inform the character of our city. Some of this is planned, some is happenstance, some is just business.

So this column is about real estate and two men: Frank Gehry and Larry Field, friends and, on occasion, partners, who shape this city. Gehry is the man of the moment; Field is best known in real estate circles. In some ways they couldn't be more different—in politics, temperament, personal interests. Yet, both are men who see, in the jumble of Los Angeles, what is real.

Real estate: Gehry builds it, transforms it, makes it usable, memorable. Field buys it, leases it, develops it. Real estate has fed their families, made them rich. Neither was born here, but both have made Los Angeles home.

Field was born in the Bronx and moved to Los Angeles in 1965. He had been in the real estate business in New York and started out by managing some downtown commercial properties. Very quickly he realized that Los Angeles was a real estate bargain. Even in the best areas, such as Mid-Wilshire, commercial property sold for ten dollars per square foot while in New York comparable properties went for twenty-five to forty dollars per square foot. He also realized that Los Angeles was one of those cities, like New York, that people from all over the country and all over the world moved to when they had made money elsewhere. Over the last thirty years he has developed more than 1 million square feet, primarily on the Westside. His company is called NSB, and Field is often heard to say "not so bad," which is exactly how he has done.

Around the beginning of 1977, Field bought two square blocks of commercial property on Main Street in Venice, seven and a half acres, for $1 million. One day, he got a call from a young architect, Gehry, who wanted to buy a parcel of the Venice property. That's how they first met.

For his part, Gehry moved to Los Angeles from Canada with his family as a teenager. Although he went east to MIT to study, he wasn't interested in playing by East Coast rules. He came back to Los Angeles and eventually settled in Santa Monica, where he lives to this day.

At that time, art collector Fred Weisman wanted Gehry to build an art museum to house his collection. In no time, Weisman, Gehry and Field joined together to develop the parcel as museum, commercial space and below market artist's studios. However the Jewish community from the Venice synagogue came out in force against them saying they threatened the senior citizens' community. They abandoned the project. Field' s property became home to Gold's Gym, The Rose Café and the Gas Company building. Gehry eventually sold his parcel to Jay Chiat who in turn had Gehry build the Venice landmark, the Chiat/Day Building, which many (including my daughter) call "the binoculars building."

A few years later, when Gehry and artist Chuck Arnoldi wanted to buy a building at Brooks, they asked Field to be a partner in return for investing his money. Field explained that Gehry didn't need him; the bank would finance the purchase. As Gehry says today, "He could have been greedy. He could have inserted himself. He didn't. He was very generous."

Field and Gehry became friends. Field does not know many artists; Gehry does not socialize with many real estate developers. Their friendship allows them to speak honestly and openly to each other about family and work — about things that are real.

Now, more than thirty years later, they are finally partners in a real estate deal. When Gehry needed new offices, he called Field. Field found them a giant Playa Vista warehouse that BMW used to own. Gehry took the back half and has his offices there and is designing the front as two office spaces—there are many Gehry design touches—an interior street between the front and back halves, a garden and a cafe (which will be run by Field's daughter, Lisa, who has a catering firm). The front offices are under construction and will be ready by January. At the same time, Gehry has asked Field to be a director in his new company, Gehry Technologies (the design software Gehry pioneered).

"After all these years, I wanted to give something back to Larry," Gehry said recently.

Field looks at real estate and he sees what could be there. Gehry is famous for using everyday materials: chain link, plywood, cardboard. He has made metal curve in ways even Uri Geller could not have imagined. Both men have had an enormous impact on the character of the Westside. They are able to see what sometimes we can't or what we take for granted. They make it real.

October 24, 2003

Reading Something into Some Books

Marboro Books, Richard Farina and Daniel Deronda

At fourteen, I had never read a book outside of school assignments—certainly not for pleasure. I was more of a comic book kid. My parents were concerned and even asked one of my friends to talk to me. I just wasn't interested.

But I liked hanging out at Marboro books in Manhattan. Marboro was a New York book chain that sold books and posters and had large tables with discounted books stacked on them, many for ninety-nine cents. There were piles of art books, coffee-table books and Victorian erotica, a very good way to encourage browsing in a teenager.

I spent hours studying *The Art of the Limerick*—poetry for adolescents of all ages. To this day, ply me with enough vodka and I may start recalling memorized couplets about complicated couplings.

In my teen years, also known as the meta-spastic era, parents were more concerned about grades than child safety, hence the expression: "You do better in that class or your father will kill you." I think my mother actually said, "disappointed," which in my home was worse than death.

As a corollary, teenagers roamed Manhattan unsupervised, mini-Lewis and Clarks searching to chart the territory and hoping to make discoveries. One particular afternoon found me making my way up Third Avenue, past Woolworth's, Alexander's and Bloomingdale's. I wandered into Marboro.

On that particular afternoon, one of the long-haired college students working there started talking to me. He asked me what kind of books I liked. I said I didn't know.

He asked if I had read *Catcher in the Rye* and did I like it? Of course. But who didn't?

He explained that school could only teach you certain things. There was an alternative education out there, and those were things you needed to teach yourself. He gave me three books to read—a sort of anti-establishment trilogy: Aldous Huxley's *Brave New World,* George Orwell's *1984* and Richard Farina's *Been Down So Long it Looks Like Up to Me,* which he described as Holden finally goes to college.

I never saw that book clerk again. The next time I went in he was gone. But I read those novels. And after that, I never stopped reading.

I read all of Huxley. My favorite was *After Many a Summer Dies the Swan*, which given that it is a novel devoted to a comic look at Hollywood narcissism, seems prescient of my current interests and affectations. I read more Orwell and every spring until I went to college I re-read *Been Down So Long.*

Farina made me want to be a writer. Although I've never thought about it—until this moment as I write this—there's a bit of Farina in my columns.

There is a great debate about how kids learn and who they learn from. To what extent do we attribute genetics, how much influence do teachers or curriculum have, what role do peers play in what we learn?

Regardless of where you come out on this, we are all, to one extent or another, autodidacts, self-taught, self-invented—and, in the long haul, it is not just what we are taught that is important but what sticks with us, what we remember.

A guy in a bookstore started me on a lifetime of reading. If my life were broken down into episodes of *Joan of Arcadia,* I might think he was a divine messenger.

I would say it never happened again. But something like it did happen just two years ago. My wife and I were at a car wash in Santa Barbara. Another woman was waiting, and we got to talking.

She was teaching at UC Santa Barbara and finishing up her doctorate in literature. What was her thesis on? George Eliot. I told her I was a big *Middlemarch* fan—the first 400 pages are slow, but after that....

She told me I had to read *Daniel Deronda* and strangely enough I believed her. I never saw her again either.

About two months later, my mother died. As I rambled around the house in midnight insomnia bouts looking for something to read, I started in on *Daniel Deronda.* I had found no solace in contemporary work, but I became absorbed with this nineteenth-century classic.

November is Jewish book month, so let me say this: *Daniel Deronda* is one of the greatest Jewish books ever written by a non-Jew. It is two different books, one about a beautiful young woman, Gwendolen, who decides on a bad marriage, and Daniel who is tempted by Gwendolen but falls for Mirah—a Jewish woman—and gets involved in her family, even as he discovers that he is, in fact, Jewish himself.

Deronda forces us to consider the price we pay for compromise, for not following our heart. At the same time, it also ponders facing our decisions, our lives and making the best of them. At the same time, the arguments concerning assimilation, a Jewish nation and life in the Diaspora are so contemporary as to seem ripped from the pages of, well, The Jewish Journal.

Books can give direction to a fourteen-year-old, give comfort and solace to one in mourning, can explain the world at whatever age or stage of life. Seems like just yesterday, I was at Marboro books, memorizing: "There was a young man from Siam…."

November 7, 2003

Gehry Spoken Here

Disney Hall may well be Frank Gehry's crowning achievement in Los Angeles—and for good reason. Approaching The Walt Disney Concert Hall from the corner of First Street and Grand Avenue, the stainless steel walls reach into the air like a conductor's arms. The interior is even more striking, an intimate space filled with light and color. Disney Hall has every chance of becoming more than a concert hall -- it stands to become a destination. Like the Getty, which is now visited as much—if not more—for the building than the art inside, Disney Hall is sure to draw visitors who care not a whit about the music. There are public gardens on the outside. Patina restaurant has relocated to Disney Hall and will also operate a lower priced cafe. Visitors will be able to dine at both without buying tickets to a performance.

However, not everyone is a fan. A friend of mine, an architect, calls Gehry's work "ugly." He argues that architects often reflect their times and Gehry's work may reflect these times, but when all is said and done, the buildings will remain ugly. Disney Hall aside (which I believe is beautiful by any standard), it is true that Gehry's work is sometimes as much about the materials and the process—the rules he is breaking, or the very fact that he is breaking them—rather than pleasing aesthetics. In this, Gehry is in keeping with many of the artists with whom he identifies.

When I first arrived in Los Angeles, I didn't really get Gehry's work. Cardboard chairs? Harsh angles? Plywood and chain-link? Exposed pipes? Big deal. Even when I got it, I didn't appreciate it. Yet, over the years, I have found myself surrounded by Gehry's work. The more I contemplate it, the more it seeps into me. By now, I regard Gehry's work not so much as architecture as poems spoken in a language of his own, a dialect of Santa Monica, California, USA.

Most weekends offer me a mini-tour of some of Gehry's local work. Driving back from my daughter's gymnastics class, I pass by the giant Claes Oldenburg binoculars on Main Street that Gehry designed as part of the former Chiat/Day building, an act of whimsy making a statement about a business. Nearby is Edgemar, a retail complex that Gehry designed in 1988. How radical this jumble of forms must have appeared; today it seems almost conventional. Watch any child playing with blocks, and you will get how Gehry references his own childhood. As Santa Monica's Main Street passes City Hall and dead-ends into the Santa Monica Place parking lot, the shadows of parked cars can be seen through the chain link. They seem to form a painting that changes as the light plays on them. The more I look at it, the more it moves me as a work of pop art.

A meal at New York Bagel in Brentwood affords a chance to see Gehry's version of New York City's Chrysler Building hanging from the ceiling, which tickles me every time I visit there. A trip to Douglas Park brings us past Gehry's home, "the fortress" encircled by chain-link and other Gehry touches. It is easy to understand how, when Gehry first remodeled his home, neighbors were offended. Offense is also part of Gehry's vocabulary.

It is no longer popular to reference the achievements of French culture, but in Gehry's work one finds French accents, homage if you will, from the sweeping curves of Le Corbusier in Gehry's curved metal to cubism in his reassembled building blocks. Yet Gehry has absorbed these elements into his Santa Monica vernacular much as Michael McCarty (of Michael's restaurants) created a California cuisine, inspired by a Gallic reliance on fresh produce and ingredients.

For a long time, Gehry was outside the mainstream. There is no question that, at some level, he remains a rebel, at odds with his past, the establishment, looking to stick his thumb in the eye of some giant. Gehry wants, as the French say, to "epater les bourgeois."

This, too, is very Californian. People come to California to break the rules. It is a state both of the right and the left wing. It is as much the home of Proposition 13, Ronald Reagan, the recall and Arnold Schwarzenegger as it is of surf culture, millionaires in hybrid vehicles, holistic healing and Tom Hayden. What binds these disparate voices is their nonconformity and their belief in California as the place where dreams can be realized.

In moving to Los Angeles, there is a process of acclimatization. East Coast pundits can riff on "going California" with all the yoga, chai lattes and plastic surgery references—but really, understanding California is about being able to see another aesthetic: California is about choice and even chaos. As you drive down the streets, there is every style of house you can imagine, sometimes one on top of the other. This could all veer towards ugliness, a characterless and undistinguished suburban sprawl. Instead, Los Angeles is a collage, distinguished by moments of beauty, grace and even whimsy.

All this is expressed in Gehry's work. Much of what he pioneered—metal roofs and glass fronts, exposed pipes, lofts and boxes, are now commonplace. Gehry is of Los Angeles: his works speaks of the territory and for the city. The time has come to claim Gehry as our own. Maybe we should post a sign: Gehry spoken here.

November 20, 2003

A Search for Intellectual LA

Paul Holdengraber and LACMA

It's a Friday night and an overflow crowd is jammed into the penthouse of the former May Co. store on Wilshire Boulevards—now Los Angeles County Museum of Art (LACMA) Wests—to hear a conversation between French journalist and philosopher Bernard-Henri Levy and The New Yorker's Adam Gopnik.

Presiding over this abundance of intelligence is Paul Holdengräber, the founder and director of LACMA's Institute for Art and Cultures (IAC). Holdengräber is erudite, worldly, self-deprecating and all the more charming for being so, equal parts Joel Grey in *Cabaret,* and Humphrey Bogart in *Casablanca.*

As a swimmer in the shallower pools of life in Los Angeles, there is something shocking (and exciting) about all these people hungry to hear intellectuals go at it in the Southland. It makes you want to ask: who is Paul Holdengräber and what is he doing in Los Angeles?

Holdengräber often describes his position as being akin to the "art of the dinner party" and his goal, he told me recently, is nothing more or less than to animate the intellectual life of Los

Angeles. In many ways, this is the perfect job for Holdengräber —if it didn't exist he would have had to invent it. Actually, as matter of fact, he did.

Five years ago, Holdengräber, then a fellow at the Getty Research Institute, approached LACMA about creating an institute for art and culture. He argued that a museum should not be a mausoleum, that it should have an intellectual mission.

"I wanted to expand the definition of 'museum,'" he said. Holdengräber argued that just as curators exhibited talented visual artists, he wanted to bring some of the most articulate thinkers, critics and writers to engage in debate and create a public forum for ideas about art and culture. LACMA decided to give Holdengräber a shot and the IAC was born.

Since 1998, Holdengräber has hosted conversations with Pierre Boulez and Frank Gehry, Esa-Pekka Salonen, Peter Sellars, Susan Sontag, Pico Iyer, André Aciman, R.B. Kitaj and David Hockney. The institute hosts a dozen events a year.

Many, like the evening I attended, are sold out. The crowd is a mix of old and young, Eastside and Westside, industry and civilian. Just this week, on December 4, former Talking Head and multimedia artist David Byrne gave a presentation, "I Love PowerPoint."

In many ways, Holdengräber's position is the culmination of his upbringing and education. The son of Viennese Jews who fled Austria before the Anschluss, only to find refuge first in Haiti and then in Mexico, Holdengräber spent much of his formative years on the move, living in Mexico, Switzerland, Austria, Belgium and France.

He studied law and philosophy at Louvain in Belgium and earned a doctorate in comparative literature at Princeton, before teaching for several years at Williams, the University of Miami and Claremont College. He arrived in Los Angeles in 1995.

Holdengräber, raised in the old world, has brought his sensibilities to the new world. Although he would have loved to have been among the cafes of Vienna at the start of the 20th century—to have known Schnitzler and Zweig—he sees his current position as the opportunity to make Los Angeles a forum for ideas of the twenty-first century. "For once, I'm in the right city at the right time," he said.

"Los Angeles," Holdengräber said, "is a work in progress. You have to expend effort." To make it work, he said, "you have to interact."

That, in a nutshell, is Holdengräber's mission—to make us interact, to engage, to inspire us, as he puts it so well, "to pursue the journey of knowing."

As we all know, it is easy to be complacent in Los Angeles. The entertainment industry can reduce one's spectrum to a world of pitches and spec scripts, of hot manuscripts and trade-related gossip focusing on who's in and who's out at the agencies and studios. What appears in *Variety* and *The Hollywood Reporter* drives the conversation, fueling an inner life that swings between envy and schadenfreude. That world can be stifling.

Some weeks it seems that the search for intellectual life in Los Angeles is limited to getting a copy of the Paris Hilton video. Although now that I've managed to work the tape into this column, I would like to say one thing to Mr. Solomon and Ms. Hilton: Used to be all a nice Jewish boy and his shiksa goddess girlfriend had to do to piss off their parents was show up at their parents' home for dinner—boy oh boy, have you two raised the stakes!

In any event, over the last year in writing this column, I have discovered another Los Angeles—Friday luncheons for fellows of the LA Institute for the Humanities, panels at the Skirball, the Villa Aurora and UCLA LIVE's ever-more eclectic programs. Each, in its own way, is altering the consciousness of Los Angeles.

Holdengräber wants his LACMA debates "to act as an aphrodisiac." Who can argue with that?

December 5, 2003

‘Fabulous Invalid’

Ruth Seymour’s Chanukah Program on KCRW

I used to have this Thanksgiving Day ritual in New York: no matter what I was doing, or where I was going, I would find a way to be near a radio around 11:30 a.m., to tune in to WNEW-FM 102.7’s broadcast of Arlo Guthrie’s “Alice’s Restaurant,” in its entirety, in all its musical and comedic glory.

Over the last few years in Los Angeles, I’ve acquired a similar accidentally/on purpose habit: every year around this time, I manage to stumble onto Ruth Seymour’s annual Chanukah tribute to Yiddish, “Philosophers, Fiddlers & Fools,” on KCRW-FM 89.9. This year the show will air on December 19, from noon to 3:00 p.m. It’s the twenty-fifth anniversary program.

Radio is a very personal medium, and to be driving around in the bright sunshine and suddenly happen upon a Yiddish song from the days of the Second Avenue Theater—or hear a short story by a Yiddish master—is surreal. But the show is so personal, so eclectic, so compelling, that on more than one occasion I’ve found myself waiting in the parking lot to hear the end of a song or rushing back to my car after a meeting to hear what Seymour would play next.

Seymour's credentials as a Yiddishist are impeccable: as a young girl growing up in the Bronx, she attended school at Sholem Aleichem; later at the City College of New York she studied under the great Yiddish scholar Max Weinreich. Back then, Seymour feared for the future of the language. However, Weinreich said to her: "Yiddish is magic. It will outlive history."

Seymour joined KCRW in 1977, when the radio signal barely broadcast beyond Hollywood and their offices were located at John Adams Middle School—you had to cross the playground to enter the station. In 1978, Seymour, feeling that in a society that is overwhelmingly Christmas-oriented "we should do something for Chanukah," created a program whose format has remained consistent to this day.

Regardless of when Chanukah begins, the show is always on a Friday so Seymour can wish her listeners a "good yontif" (happy holiday—a traditional greeting for the Sabbath and holidays). The first part is traditional folk music—and the selections are often eclectic with recordings from the United States, Romania, France and Canada.

The second part is a memorial section where Seymour plays such songs as the Warsaw Ghetto Partisan's song, "Zog Nit Kayn Mol" (Never Say), as well as "Ani Ma'amin" (I Believe). She always ends this section by reading the final page of Andre Schwarz-Bart's elegiac novel, *The Last of the Just.*

The third is a dramatic reading of a short story. One of the highlights, Seymour recalled, was the year Lauren Bacall read *A Ghetto Dog* by Isaiah Spiegel. This year, Theodore Bikel will read the late Isaac Bashevis Singer's *Androgynous,* which was recently published in *The New Yorker.*

The final hour is what Seymour calls "the Second Avenue Hit Parade," where she plays many of the old chestnuts—songs so familiar you forgot you even still knew them.

For Seymour, Yiddish remains the language of exile, of the galut (Diaspora)—it is the mamaloshen (the mother tongue). The program is a chance to share her heritage, which has informed a great part of her character. The Chanukah program, Seymour confesses, is "a love letter to my own childhood."

The irony is that when Seymour first conceived the show, Yiddish seemed to be disappearing. Today there are more recordings than ever. The Milken Archive of American Jewish Music has just released *Great Songs from the Yiddish Stage: Abraham Ellstein (1907-1963)*. That this CD is marked "Volume 1" speaks volumes in and of itself.

Need more evidence of a resurgence of Yiddish? This week, the California Institute for Yiddish Culture and Language in Marina del Rey is offering intensive classes in language and culture as well as a December 20 concert at UCLA featuring Bikel.

Earlier I mentioned Singer's passing because you wouldn't guess it by his literary output. Since his death in 1991, Singer has published several novels, including my dream film project, "Shadows on the Hudson," and many short stories. Frankly, I am equal parts jealous and annoyed that Singer has published more dead than I probably will alive. The whole point of dying is that other people get a turn—in estate law they have "The Rule Against Perpetuities." But apparently not at Singer's publishing house.

That being said, it is worth noting that Singer's "new" publications (originally published in Yiddish in the Forverts), reveal an earthier, darker side than his American image as a grandfatherly imp, the Yiddish Yoda. For example, *Shadows* is the underside of *Enemies: A Love Story*—a novel of "Survivors Gone Wild" in the New World. Similarly, *Androgynous* can be seen as the darker version of *Yentl*—not a woman who wants to be a man, but a woman who is both a man and a woman.

Nonetheless, Seymour still has cause for concern: she is worried about Yiddish being used as a marketing ploy in countries without Jews. Also, when the show first aired, "this one program received more mail than any other during the rest of the year combined. That," she admits, "has diminished."

"I no longer feel I am single-handedly keeping Yiddish alive," Seymour says, "Now, it's just a Chanukah program."

Let me correct Seymour: it's not just a Chanukah show—it's a tradition, accidentally/on purpose. As for keeping the magic of Yiddish alive, Bikel said it best: "Yiddish is like the theater, 'the fabulous invalid,' always dying, never dead."

December 19, 2003

Dreaming of a Blue and White Christmas

Christmas Movies from Michael Curtiz to Jon Favreau

Christmas came early this year—November. 7, when New Line Cinema released *Elf,* the family-friendly comedy that, as of this writing, has earned more than $156 million. Another surprise is the success of the far-more-cynical adult offering *Bad Santa,* which had a production cost of $18 million and, since its November 26 release, has earned more than $43 million. These are Christmas films that, you could say, are good for the Jews. Both are written and directed by persons of the Jewish faith. *Elf* is directed (Jon Favreau), written by (David Berenbaum) and has stars (James Caan, Edward Asner) who are Jewish—a rare trifecta, particularly for a Christmas film—a feat that parallels the success of the 1954 *White Christmas* (Michael Curtiz, Norm Krasna and Danny Kaye, respectively).

Accordingly, you might wonder, as I do, in Carrie Bradshaw fashion: Did the Jews invent Christmas movies, or is making Christmas movies a way for Jews to reinvent themselves?

I grew up in a family where Christmas made my parents nervous. As December slid toward January, we were inevitably on edge, listening hard for the sound of pounding hooves or polished jackboots goose-stepping down the avenue that would announce the coming pogrom. Or maybe that was just me and my imagination. My Holocaust-refugee parents never really talked about their feelings.

In any event, I have a love/hate relationship with Christmas—I like the spirit, the feeling of fellowship and the parties. But all that enforced cheer and caroling and people drinking too much makes me uncomfortable, even when I'm one of them. Let's be clear about one thing: if eggnog were that good, people would drink it year-round. Still, as best I can, as a twenty-first century Jew, I try to feel the love at Christmastime.

Growing up, our own Christmas ritual was simple: we got up early, wandered up Fifth Avenue (no crowds) to see the windows at Saks and the other stores (which were closed, so no shopping) and then we made our way to an afternoon movie.

This brings us back to Christmas movies. So many of them; so many made by Jews. On the one hand it would be easy to explain the phenomenon as "just a job"—just "working for the man." But let's face it, a hundred years ago in the nascent film industry, as Neal Gabler's *Empire of Their Own*, makes clear "the man" was circumcised.

In the history of the Jewish Christmas movie, I discern three separate periods, each revealing of its era. The first is the age of "the dream factory," where Jewish immigrant movie moguls, eager to leave the Old World behind, became more American than the Americans: names changed, customs changed. For that first generation, creating Christmas stories was an affirmation of their ability to put a gloss on the mainstream culture and sell it to itself.

At the same time, the movies codified a secular version of Christmas as a picture-perfect event, complete with fireplace, stockings, mistletoe and children scurrying about—part Norman Rockwell, part Currier & Ives. It was assimilation in the purest sense—not as it is so often portrayed, as an attempt to deny their own past—but proof of how well they understood American culture. It was aspirational. They were creating what they thought America hoped to see when they looked in the mirror.

The second phase is epitomized by *White Christmas*, both the song and the movie. In the 1920s and 1930s another wave of Jewish émigrés came to Hollywood. They, too, changed their names. Many of them also left their past behind. They were mainly directors and actors, among them Billy Wilder, Leslie Howard and Michael Curtiz, who not only directed *Casablanca* but *White Christmas* as well. *White Christmas* was first born as a song written by Irving Berlin (né Izzy Baline in Siberia) for the 1942 film *Holiday Inn*. Wishing for an idealized world, "I used to know" that's "merry and bright," the lyrics are, at the same time, wistful, hopeful and all-inclusive. The song was so popular (it is one of the most popular songs of all time), it spawned a movie of its own.

The movie *White Christmas* pairs *Der Bingle* Bing Crosby with the very versatile Kaye in a romantic musical comedy about two World War II veterans who achieve success in show business and then success in love. Its message is not religious, but universal.

Curtiz presents the world as it was and as it should be. Curtiz, like Berlin, was often critiqued for having no signature style. But for Curtiz and Berlin's generation, being able to work successfully in any number of styles was a virtue unto itself. Making a Christmas movie was not about assimilation, it was about versatility. Curtiz had already assimilated back in Hungary when he first changed his name from Mano Kaminer to Mihaly Kertesz (a more Hungarian-sounding name). The jump from Kertesz to Curtiz was itself a testament to having an identity that was easily translated—that worked, literally and figuratively, in any culture. America was the land of freedom, and it was a country where you could do anything, even make a Christmas movie.

We are now in phase three. Born in America, the second-, third- and fourth-generation of Jews in Hollywood were raised during a time when institutional anti-Semitism had all but disappeared and where assimilation was not so much a goal as a norm. The melting pot has given way to the multicultural quilt—and religious choice is as varied as the combo plates on a Chinese menu. Although Jews are still making Christmas movies, the reasons for doing so are as diverse as the movies made.

In the past, Jews played the non-Jewish roles. Today, in a sign of how Jewish culture has permeated popular culture, last weekends' No. 1 hit, *Something's Got to Give* has Diane Keaton playing a Jewish woman and Frances McDormand plays her sister. Oy!

For its part, *Elf* harks back to the "secular" Christmas movie. It is about Santa, reindeer, the joy of song—it is about "the Christmas Spirit." The carpenter of Nazareth gets nary a mention. *Elf* leaves the "Christ" out of Christmas. Favreau does appear in one scene as a doctor and lest you think he has completely forsaken the Maccabees, there is a menorah on the shelf behind him.

More to the point, Favreau has now joined the club of directors whose movies have broken the one hundred million dollar barrier. Success is power. Today's Hollywood belongs to no religion—save a corporate one. The first generation owned the studios. Today they are owned by corporations and controlled in great part by non-Jews. Although there are many Jewish executives, they are merely employees, serving at the whim of the marketplace and their masters. According to lore, the Jews in ancient Egypt built the pyramids—but does anyone consider the pyramids Jewish? Nonetheless what is remarkable about this era is that filmmakers can now express how uncomfortable Christmas makes them. Last year, Larry David, our poet laureate of discomfort, milked his resentment of Christmas into a hysterical and embarrassing episode of *Curb Your Enthusiasm*, "Mary, Joseph and Larry."

Still nothing prepared me for *Bad Santa*, written and directed by Terry Zwigoff, a movie where the self-loathing hits toxic and keeps going. There are some very funny bits, and there also some moments when you just can't believe what you just heard or saw on screen. Yet, there have been no major protests concerning this desecration of holiday traditions—most likely because the attack is on the secular Christmas, not the religious.

Finally, the twenty-first century has been witness to a landmark event: the release of the first animated Chanukah feature-length movie, Adam Sandler's *Eight Crazy Nights*. Personally, I find Sandler's cretin-savant aesthetic endearing because, although his mind may be trapped in adolescence, his heart inevitably is in the right place. That and he's wicked funny. So phase three, it turns out, is about options. When we turn on the television or go to the multiplex, we the see the ghosts of Jewish Christmas movies past, present and future. These represent the world as it might be, as we wish it was and as it is—both good and bad. There have always been and will always be Christmas movies and, in a true democracy, Jews will continue to make them, just as non-Jews will make films from Jewish material. And each film will, for each generation, serve as a sign of how far we have come, and of where we are at. Happy Holidays.

December 26, 2003

When Television Challenged America

Rod Serling

Around this time of year, I'm often prone to recall Rod Serling, who was born on Christmas Day. I'm helped along by the fact that PBS ran their *American Masters* portrait of Serling over the New Year's weekend even as the Sci-Fi Channel ran a *Twilight Zone* marathon. It makes me wonder: Where is Serling—or today's Serling—when you really need him?

My interest in Serling is professional as well as personal: For the last several years, together with writers Ron Magid and Paul Clemens, I've been trying to produce a Serling biopic in partnership with producer Steve Rubin and Serling's widow, Carol.

What I find so compelling about Serling is this: It's 1950s Eisenhower America and the country has been lulled into a false sense of comfort by Betty Crocker images of the happy and prosperous American middle-class family. But Serling knows different.

Raised in upstate New York, one of the few Jews in Binghampton, he served as a paratrooper in the Pacific, and returned home suffering from nightmares about his service there. A driven writer, he wanted to wake up America to another reality: He wanted Americans to know about lynchings in the South, about the Holocaust, about the possibility of nuclear destruction. TV networks and their advertisers didn't want controversy; they wanted audiences. But Serling conceived a way to get his message across, using science fiction. Serling created *The Twilight Zone*, transforming the medium and its viewers.

Over the course of five seasons, Serling poured out his heart and soul, driving himself to near creative exhaustion. As host and narrator, he kept the show on the air by being its pitchman, gaining fame but almost selling his soul in the process. By the time *The Twilight Zone* went off the air in 1965, a different America was dawning—an America that had witnessed nuclear tests, the Bay of Pigs and President Kennedy's assassination… an America that would soon be marching in the streets to protest civil rights and the war in Vietnam.

Prior to Serling, neither news nor entertainment programming exposed America's real crises. Now that the news was finally conveying the reality that Serling wanted to reveal, Americans sought refuge from those darker truths in sitcoms, escaping to *Gilligan's Island*.

To some extent we've been escaping since. Despite the nomenclature of "reality" TV, current programming has little to do with reality. The one-hour dramas that I so enjoy are as escapist as sitcoms. They, too, provide comfort, in their way, from today's realities. *CSI: Crime Scene Investigation* and its offspring tell us that evidence prevails, that O.J. to the contrary, forensics trap criminals. And, as Saddam exits his spider hole and Osama continues to bedevil us, *Cold Case* and *Without a Trace* (one of my favorite shows) let us know that evil-doers will be caught no matter how long it takes, and that the missing will be searched for—all antidotes to the fear trafficked in by local newscasts and tabloid headlines.

Some shows provide windows into our fears and neuroses: *24* is particularly adept at taking our greatest fears and heightening them beyond a point we ever imagined; *The O.C.* reports on teenage angst; and *Joan of Arcadia* brings God, if not spirituality, into the conversation. But these shows, as good as they are, do not challenge us to improve the world we encounter. That is what *The Twilight Zone*, at its best, accomplished.

This is not to say that no shows have tried to reach Serling's standard. The *Law & Order* franchise boasts plots "ripped from the headlines," but they are exploiting facts, not deepening our understanding of them. Aaron Sorkin's *West Wing* certainly had the passion and the will to tackle issues but somehow those efforts appeared, even while watching, quixotic. In recent memory, perhaps *The X-Files* came closest, but while they occasionally walked up to the line of truth and provocation, they never dared to cross it as Serling did over and over.

I won't argue that every episode of *The Twilight Zone* was transcendent—many were just gimmicky. Serling, however, set a precedent—that television could be subversive—it could entertain, inform and take on the status quo, all the while asking us to be better than we are. It was ambitious.

Maybe that's no longer possible. Perhaps television has changed too much.

Perhaps there are too many channels chasing too segmented an audience. Maybe it is the audience that has changed into a country that thinks politics are too personal a subject to discuss out loud—except as entertainment on talk radio and other quasi-news programs. If television can manage to comfort us, distract us and even entertain us, isn't that more than enough? Serling said no.

At the start of a new year, it's a good time to remember Serling and to recall that one driven man could, by the mere force of his writing, wake up America.

January 9, 2004

The Diving Desert

Palm Springs, The Desert, and Deanne Stillman's Twentynine Palms

As I write this, it's sixty-four degrees in Santa Monica and Sub-Zero is just a brand of refrigerator I covet. On the East Coast, there is a record cold spell and everyone is paying rapt attention to the wind-chill factor.

The climatic difference can best be explained not merely by boasting or gloating—but by the fact that Los Angeles is a desert.

For most Angelenos, heading out to the desert means driving on the 10 for about two hours to reach the desert communities, so-called: Palm Springs, Cathedral City, Palm Desert, and La Quinta. Here the desert blooms green with golf courses and condos.

In some ways, the relationship between the desert and Los Angeles is as if some mad scientist had extracted variant strains from the local culture and seeded them in its own petri dish (not unlike the relationship of the Hamptons to New York). There is the Palm Springs of the 1950s, of Frank Sinatra, Lucille

Ball, Bing Crosby and, to toss in a literary reference, Norman Mailer's *Deer Park.* You can even board an air-conditioned bus to tour the movie stars' homes. A whole cult has arisen around the architecture and furniture of the period that the more serious-minded refer to as Mid-Century. To paraphrase Mr. Eliot, in the consignment shops cool hunters come to play / speaking of houses by Richard Neutra and Albert Frey.

In downtown Palm Springs, you can feel the hipness quotient rising. Trina Turk has her first boutique there. Hotels for the hipoisie are sprouting right and left: there is the Korzen-Wearstler-designed Estrella Inn (think of it as Viceroy Jr.), the Jetson-like Orbit Inn and the Moroccan-inspired Korakia Pensione. The early adopters are buying second homes nearby. There is an enclave by the airport where trend definers like Lynda Keeler of la.com (my wife consults there) have purchased fifties desert abodes and redone them. People more wise in the ways of money than I (regrettably that's not saying much) believe Indian casino money (both people spending it and hoping to earn it) will continue to fuel the current upgrade.

This is the resort life and I'm a resort kind of guy. For Team Teicholz, that means sitting by the pool at midday in between trips down the water slide; seeing every family movie on view at the many desert multiplexes, capped by some wardrobe enhancement missions at the Cabazon premium outlet mall. There are also some excellent eating opportunities: from the breakfast at Keedy's Fountain & Grill (big on classic ambience), to Crazy Coyote Tacos in Banning, to Fleming's for steaks (I don't know why their rib-eye is better than anyone else's, it just is). I have yet to make it to Gramma's Country

Kitchen in Banning, but my fellow fressers, Eric Rahn and Rob Stavis, put it on their Top 10 breakfasts at No. 3, just behind Pasquale's in Santa Fe and the Camelia Grill in New Orleans.

However, like Los Angeles, it all depends what road you are on. Stay on Highway 111 and you are in the resort world. Take Highway 62 off the 10 and you are headed into Joshua Tree and toward Twentynine Palms. Highway 62 reveals the natural beauty of the desert, and some of the ugliness of the broken dreams that we would like to forget.

Deanne Stillman knows this world. More than any writer I know, the desert speaks to her, and she speaks for it. Stillman grew up in Cleveland, but even as a child the desert captured her imagination. After attending college in New Mexico and despite a flirtation with New York (where we first met), she made Los Angeles home. Still, the desert called to her. In articles for *The New York Times,* the *Los Angeles Times*, and *LA Weekly,* Stillman started to cover the desert. Exploring the Mojave, which she has called "this windswept museum of hope, this weird bakery of the impossible," and Joshua Tree (in her words: "the ecstatic vegetable"), she followed Highway 62 until it led to Twentynine Palms.

One day in a desert bar, she heard a story about two girls who'd been killed: Amanda Scott and Rosalie Ortega. Mandi and Rosie. Mandi was two days shy of her sixteenth birthday. Deanne asked who they were.

"Just two girls," someone said.

"They partied too hard," someone said later.

In a nightmare version of *An Officer and a Gentleman,* they had been murdered by a Marine from the local base, recently returned from the first Gulf War.

Stillman spent the next ten years researching, writing, living the trial, soaking up the desert till she had to run away—and staying away until she had to come back. The resulting book, *Twentynine Palms: A True Story of Murder, Marines, and the Mojave* (Perennial, 2002), is a true crime story in the tradition of *In Cold Blood* and the *The Executioner's Song*. They used to call it the nonfiction novel, today they call it narrative nonfiction. It's just fine writing, a searing story and tour of the desert most people prefer to avoid. She did justice to Mandi and Rosie and to the desert, as well.

So when I knew I was going to write about the desert, I called Stillman. Most people view the desert as arid and barren. To her the desert is alive in a literal way, filled with surprises from the most sublime wildflowers, to offering her a spiritual and emotional center. It is, in her words "the elusive core of Los Angeles."

The desert is what you get when you pare away the city—good and bad, high life and low life, real and fake. As Stillman told me, Joan Didion wrote about the disconnect in Los Angeles. Stillman feels it's just the opposite: the desert is the connection.

January 23, 2004

Newman Cares

Randy Newman

Are we the luckiest people in the world to live in Los Angeles, leading the lives others only dream about? Or is this the most unfair city in the nation, where the few are insulated from the harsh realities of the many? And what, you may wonder, does any of this have to do with Randy Newman?

Those are among the many questions that came to mind while attending "Shock and Awe: The Songs of Randy Newman," a recent UCLA Live event at Royce Hall. Organized by Hal Willner and Janine Nichols, an eclectic mix of mostly local artists (many of whom I did not recognize onstage) performed 46 works from Newman's canon. The featured artists included Victoria Williams, Vic Chesnutt, Ellen Greene, David Hidalgo, Howard Tate, Bob Neuwirth, Van Dyke Parks, Jon Brion and Gavin Friday. A nifty night in Los Angeles, for sure.

The next day, I went to Second Spin in Santa Monica and cleaned out their Randy Newman section.

I still remember the first time I heard "Sail Away"—a friend's older brother insisted we listen. We sat there stunned, and the album remains today just as exhilarating, clever, funny, subversive and hypnotic. Some of the lines from "Political Science" remain imprinted on my brain.

Repeated listenings this past week of the *Randy Newman Songbook Vol. 1*, "Sail Away," "Trouble in Paradise" and "Faust" produced great pleasure but also great confusion. It is hard to get a fix on Newman. His songs are detached, cynical, ambiguous, perverse, yet they seem confessional, intimate and revealing. But of what?

In "Sail Away," the narrator is a slave trader beckoning Africans to board his ship and come to America. In other tunes, Newman gives voice to rednecks, militarists and racists, and, of course, there is that song about short people. Are we supposed to see these noxious characters as alarming or ironic put-downs? In several songs, Newman takes on the persona of God, and in his play, "Faust," he sang the part of the devil (this, from an atheist). Other songs conjure up specific places or times, Louisiana, Baltimore, Capetown, Miami and LA (we love it!). The music itself conjures up distinct pictures as well, from a New Orleans second-line shuffle to a Kurt Weill/Lotte Lenye cabaret, from traditional music of the Deep South to modern pop anthems. What's it all about, Randy?

Here's what I think: Randy Newman is the songsmith of human frailty. He doesn't want to let us or himself off the hook.

Newman, in many ways, need not complain. He spent part of his youth in his mother's native New Orleans, before moving to Los Angeles. His father was a doctor, and his uncle, Alfred Newman, was music director for 20th Century Fox and the most famous film composer of all time with nine Oscars. As a teenager, Newman often visited the scoring stage at Fox to see his uncle conduct. After high school, he worked for several years writing songs in the legendary Brill Building in New York. His first album came out when he was in his mid-twenties and for more than thirty years, he's led a privileged life in Los Angeles. He's had his periods of inactivity but eventually he joined the family business—writing movie scores, contributing to *Toy Story, Ragtime, Parenthood* and *James and the Giant Peach,* among many others. He won an Oscar in 2002 for *If I Didn't Have You* from *Monsters, Inc.* Currently on any Friday night you can hear him singing *It's a Jungle Out There* over the opening credits of *Monk.* So what's there to complain about?

I think that's the point. Privilege does not give you a pass. Newman recalls seeing ice cream trucks in the South as a child that had one side for whites and the other for "colored." Newman's father told the late Timothy White, that as a kid in Los Angeles, Newman was asked by a girl to a cotillion at the Riviera Country Club. Her father called to uninvite Newman because the club didn't allow Jews. This prompted Newman to research all religions and become an atheist. As a young man, he saw that his uncle was no saint, and that great job at Fox, sometimes was just work. Newman married at an early age, raised a family. Then he found himself to be just a man—a man who, as he told one interviewer, left his wife and family for a younger woman. At an age when his own children were getting married and having children, Newman found himself starting a new family.

One recent song, "Life Isn't Fair," says it all. It opens with Newman singing about Karl Marx and Marx's dream of a better society. However, if Marx were alive today, Newman sings, he'd bring him over to his "mansion on the hill" and tell him a story that would "give his heart a chill." What's the story? It's about going to orientation at his kids' school and seeing all the beautiful moms with their husbands, like him "froggish men, unpleasant to see." (Been there, seen that!) Marx would be glad he was dead, Newman sings, because his plan just brought misery and in the land of the free, "the rich get richer/and the poor you don't ever have to see." Newman concludes: "It would depress us Karl, because we care/that the world still isn't fair."

To me, that's Newman's point. The lives we lead can insulate us from some of the injustice. But don't pretend it doesn't exist. We don't get a pass and we can't ignore it. That is life. That is man. Maybe you can't change it, but if you don't sing or talk about it, the things that humans think and do—perverse, evil or ironic as they may be—well then, the joke's on you.

Newman cares. Maybe that's why we care about him.

February 6, 2004

Conal's the Poster Boy for 'Art Attack'

Guerrilla Poster Artist Robbie Conal

You've seen them around town: a poster of a grinning, gnarly Arnold Schwarzenegger with red eyes and the words, "Achtung, Baby," scrawled in German Gothic type across his forehead. It may have made you smile; you may have felt it was in bad taste. Perhaps a bit of both. In any event, you probably thought: There goes the poster guy again.

By now, even if you can't name the artist, Robbie Conal, the style has become familiar: a black-and-white head-and-shoulders portrait made up of an agglomeration of wrinkles, blemishes, receding hairlines—the polar opposite of air-brushing—that build to define a recognizable face surrounded by words that amount to an indictment or in Conal's term, an "art attack." Over the years, few public figures of any note, from Ronald Reagan to Bill Clinton and from Tammy Faye to Martha Stewart, have dodged the brush.

About four times a year, for the last eighteen years, Conal and crew go out midnight postering, and thus far they've managed to avoid arrest—Conal's Web site, www.robbieconal.com, recommends telling police officers that "you're doing an art project." For those who prefer their Conal without a side of potential misdemeanor, his work appears on a monthly basis in the LA Weekly since 1997 and has recently been collected in a book, "ARTBURN" (RDV Books), with a foreword by Howard Zinn of "The People's History" (and yes, of Matt and Ben fame).

Conal (the name comes from Russian Jews who fled to Ireland and then to the United States where they conflated Cohen and Connally) grew up on Manhattan's Upper West Side. Conal's art education began early. His parents were union organizers, often out marching or instigating, leaving Conal, an only child, to his own devices.

They would leave a brown-bag lunch for him, a 1 dollar bill and two subway tokens, with a note to go to any art museum in the city until it closed. Such benign neglect was strangely empowering.

Conal attended P.S. 93, P.S. 118 and then the High School of Music and Art. He graduated at sixteen and then spent a brief year at Brooklyn College before heading to the West Coast, where, after a more than decade-long odyssey that had him living in the Haight, working the night shift at the post office, getting kicked out of San Francisco State for occupying school buildings as a protest, going to Canada and playing semipro baseball, getting adjudged 1-Y by the draft board (psychologically unfit to serve), returning to San Francisco to drive a Yellow Cab during the graveyard shift (he is currently writing a "comedic noir" novel about the experience) he enrolled in Stanford's master of fine arts program, where his teachers included Frank Lobdell and Nathan Olivera, the tough guys of Bay Area abstraction. But he still hadn't found his way.

With 20/20 hindsight, there were several important landmarks over the next decade that would lead to his decision to start postering.

At that time, abstract expressionism ruled. Conal was one of its adherents until he went to visit a girlfriend who was studying Renaissance art in Rome. She took him to see Michaelangelo's *Last Judgment.*

It spoke to him: "Art about the human condition—the human figure in dire straights." It seemed like something he should be addressing in his work.

The final elements in Conal's journey to becoming a guerrilla poster artist were the election and subsequent re-election of Ronald Reagan. Reagan, you could say, made Conal the artist he is today.

Reading the newspaper during the early eighties, Conal "found steam coming out of my eyes, ears, nose and throat." In "Art Attack," a now out-of-print book that collected Conal's posters between 1986 and 1992, Conal describes his 1986 Archimedes moment: "I'd just stare at Reagan, Regan, Weinberger, James Baker III, Shultz and Casey. Suddenly, I found myself making nasty little portraits of ugly old white men with pursed lips—okay, no lips. And it came together—this tight little club of power-mongers were: MEN WITH NO LIPS."

Conal wanted his work to reach the public. That wasn't going to happen by showing in art galleries. Instead, he decided to translate his work into posters and "hit the street."

There was one hitch: Conal knew nothing about making

posters. But the first baseman on his Sunday softball team, John Berley, did—he was a printer.

Conal spent 600 dollars for 1,000 posters that featured four portraits, each with a word beneath the face: Reagan (MEN), Regan (WITH), Weinberger (NO) and Baker (LIPS). Conal and his friend, Lenny Silverberg, went out late one night in Conal's Honda Civic wagon filled with posters, brushes and pots of glue, following a basic route between Conal's studio in Venice (at 5th and Rose avenues) and his mother's apartment in Park La Brea.

Reagan had been dubbed "The Teflon President," because no scandal stuck to him. Conal decided instead to stick it to Reagan. Conal deliberately placed posters at traffic switch boxes, where drivers would see them.

Los Angeles has always been a semioticians' paradise, where people are attuned to every sign, from which car you drive to the thickness of your yoga mat. They noticed. People weren't sure what the posters meant or whose agenda or product they were pushing. But Conal knew he was on to something.

Men With No Lips was followed by *Women With Teeth* (Nancy Reagan, Margaret Thatcher, Jeanne Kirkpatrick and Joan Rivers). By the third poster, Ollie North (CONFESS), Conal had found his voice, his medium, his métier.

Conal, the former art brat, had tapped into a tradition reaching back to Goya and that referenced Kathe Kollwitz, Georg Grosz and the Mexican muralists Orozco and Rivera. To see Conal's work in art-historical context, you need do little more than walk into the UCLA Hammer Museum in Westwood and check out their collection of drawings and busts by Daumier. Even today, the portraits are simultaneously entertaining and damning.

Over the years, Conal's haiku-like commentary on our times has often captured the zeitgeist. Some of my favorites include a portrait of Reagan with the words: "Contra" above his face and "Diction" below; Jim Bakker and Tammy Faye with the words, "False Profit"; and George H. W. Bush with the phrase, "It can't happen here," written so that "here" is on his forehead.

Among the most notorious is a portrait of then-LA Police Chief Daryl Gates' head superimposed on a rifle target. Writ large is a quote from Gates: "Casual drug users should be taken out and shot"—Conal took a blue grease pen, crossed out "shot" and wrote "Beaten," a reference to Rodney King. Love it or hate it, fair or unfair, it remains one of Conal's most powerful works.

Carol Wells of the Center for the Study of Political Graphics, says: "Conal has made the political poster his own."

Conal is unique, she says, in that his work is "half-art, half-protest." Most distinctive, Wells feels is Conal's use of humor. His provocative and at times ambiguous word play is all the more powerful, she says, because it makes you "look at the world a little differently."

Conal's monthly cartoon/column in the *LA Weekly* has allowed him to experiment with larger blocks of text and make more direct commentary on events and subjects in the news, such as Clinton, Colin Powell, Dick Cheney and Stewart.

Part of Conal would like to retire from the art attacks. It's been 18 years, but, as Conal says, "Stuff keeps happening." In fact, as election season heats up, Conal's planning an anti-Bush project, which will be a collaborative artwork with two other young artists, Sheperd Fairey of "Obey Giant" fame, and LA Graffiti writer Mear. They plan on doing a triptych, with each doing a portrait with text.

Conal has been criticized for making his subjects ugly. Although one could argue that by fifty, everyone gets the face they deserve, or that the face tells the story of the soul, or that "ugly" art has a long history and is part of the aesthetic Conal imbued from his teachers at Stanford. Whether in response to this criticism or not, Conal has recently done some inspirational images that have a beauty rarely found in his earlier work.

After September 11, Conal was approached by Jim Otis, a filmmaker who is devoted to the principles of nonviolence, to do portraits of inspiration. Conal was concerned about the dangers of overreaction to the World Trade Center bombing, or as Chris Rock put it in his current stand-up tour, about "Patriotism becoming hate-triotism."

Conal drew portraits of Ghandi, the Dalai Lama and the Rev. Martin Luther King Jr., with the words for each, "Waiting, Watching, Dreaming." Once the posters went up, it was as if these modern-era apostles of nonviolence were standing on street corners watching how we behaved.

More recently, guerrilla poster crew member and actor David Arquette suggested Conal do a series about musicians who've inspired us and commissioned a portrait of John Lennon. Bob Marley and others are to follow in the series. All through my interview with Conal, I kept thinking of that other master of the multiple, Andy Warhol. Although Warhol's work was thought to be consciously apolitical, similarities kept popping into mind. Both artists sought to transmute popular culture and create a dissonance that would serve as commentary.

Consider Warhol's early work, *Electric Chairs,* and even his later portraits of Mao. Warhol was famous for his commissioned portraits—and his commissioned series, such as *Famous Jews of the 20th Century.* Warhol also collaborated with younger artists, most notably with Basquiat.

Despite the similarities, the more I thought about it, the more I realized Conal is the anti-Warhol. Warhol made art of the shallow; Conal makes art by showing us the shallowness of the high and mighty. Warhol, on occasion, made art that had a political dimension. Conal's art is politics.

February 27, 2004

Schindler's Impact

The 10th Anniversary of Schindler's List

In May 1995, I found myself in Lviv, Ukraine. My father had died two years before; and I was there on a roots trip. I wanted to see the city where he grew up and perhaps unearth some of the information that he could never bring himself to share, such as the names and birthdates of his brothers and sisters, all murdered. I discovered his own real birthday to be a completely different day, month and year than we had always celebrated.

On that day, I visited a hill outside a prison camp that was likely where his parents and brothers and sisters were murdered, as a reprisal for his having escaped from the ghetto. It was another fact that I had only learned since his death. I said "Kaddish" and went back to my hotel to collapse, emotionally spent.

That night, alone in my hotel room, I channel surfed. Suddenly, there before my eyes was a black-and-white nightclub scene that pulled back to reveal Liam Neeson dubbed in Russian. *Schindler's List* was being broadcast for the first time on Russian TV (bootleg tapes had circulated but the movie had never been on TV). This was the first time most Ukrainians would see the film. I was transfixed.

I understood little of what was being said in Russian, but freed from the language I was enthralled with the images and their emotional manipulation. Tears started rolling down my cheeks. I don't remember the movie ending; I don't remember turning the TV off; I don't remember falling asleep.

The next morning, I spoke with people at the hotel, at the Central archives in a church—they had all watched *Schindler's* the night before and were moved. One young woman said to me, "I thought I knew. I didn't. I thought I understood. I didn't." That's when I realized the importance of *Schindler's List,* its ability to permeate the consciousness of people in Lviv, Ukraine.

When I first heard that Steven Spielberg was set to make a film version of Thomas Keneally's *Schindler's Ark*—the special 10th anniversary of edition *Schindler's List* comes out this week—I worried. I feared that in the story of Oskar Schindler, Spielberg, like Keneally, had found a gentile prism, rather than a Jewish one, through which to tell the horrific events of the Holocaust era. Although Oskar Schindler saved more than 1,000 Jewish lives during the Holocaust, there were many aspects of his story that bothered me. There was something offensive about the paternalistic attitude of Schindler toward "his Jews." Conversely, the devotion of the Schindlerjuden to him, basically supporting him for the rest of his life, seemed like an unhealthy Stockholm syndrome-like reaction. But that was not my biggest concern. I worried that the story of Schindler would be misleading, that the emphasis would be on Schindler and not the Jews.

"For one Oskar Schindler, how many collaborators were there?" Elie Wiesel once wrote in *TV Guide*. Schindler and the others deemed "the Righteous" and "the Just" stand out because they were the exceptions to human behavior during those dark years. As Wiesel noted, in his own Holocaust experience there were no Schindlers: "None of the Just crossed my path during the war. None of our Christian neighbors in my small village of Sighet, in Romania, risked his life to take in, to hide, to rescue a Jewish child or Jewish friend."

I worried that the story of Schindler, rather than showing the truth of what occurred, would create a dangerous myth: That not only were non-Jews in Poland not complicit in the murders, but regular people, Nazi Party members like Oskar Schindler, saved Jews—Jews who were too weak, too powerless, too lacking in any heroism to even save themselves. This would be a slur on the survivors and a second death for the murdered. Such is the problem of making an example of the exceptional.

Then I saw the film and all my reservations disappeared. I succumbed to the power of the movie making. It was as if Spielberg had used all the tools at his disposal to tell a compelling and engrossing story. He checked his ego at the door and let the story be the star. It was an amazing achievement: Spielberg used Liam Neeson as the handsome gentile to seduce the audience into caring, much as Schindler seduced the Nazis into saving lives. It was a valid way, even a commercial way, to tell the story of the Holocaust. For once he had not made a Spielberg film. For that he received an Oscar. For that the film went on to make a fortune. Spielberg used the money to fund the Survivors of the Shoah Foundation—once again, reaching beyond himself to make something that would have a lasting impact on others.

But I still didn't grasp the full impact of the film until that evening in my hotel room in Ukraine.

Schindler rescued 1,100 men, women and children—"his workers," "his people." In connection with Schindler, the talmudic saying is often quoted that "whoever saves one life, saves the entire world." What then can we say about Spielberg who opened the hearts and minds of millions? An estimated 50 million people worldwide saw *Schindler's List* in movie theaters, and 65 million watched it when it was first broadcast on television.

While there are only 13 million Jews in the world, Rabbi Steven Leder of Wilshire Boulevard Temple said, Spielberg with one film shed light on the Holocaust to more than 100 million non-Jews. "I find that staggering in its importance."

Annette Insdorf, author of I*ndelible Shadows: Film and the Holocaust,* the definitive and essential tome on the subject, feels *Schindler's List* also made it easier for Holocaust films to get made, because, as she wrote me by e-mail, "despite the difficult subject matter, hefty running time and choice of black and white, it had both commercial and critical success." In the recently published third edition, which looks to be about three times as thick as the first, Insdorf notes that since her last update in 1989, she's seen approximately 170 Holocaust-related films. As she notes in her introduction to the third edition, "The number of cinematic reconstructions—fictional as well as documentary—is staggering. They both reflect and contribute to the fact that awareness has replaced silence about the Shoah."

Further, in founding the Survivors of the Shoah Visual History Foundation, Spielberg has dramatically increased our storehouse of knowledge. The recording of 52,000 Holocaust survivors' testimonies is a great accomplishment, a monumental resource for historians, students—it gives succor and satisfaction to Holocaust survivors and their families, that their experiences are recorded for history for posterity. At best it gives lie to the intention of the Nazis and their henchmen that their crimes and the lives they plundered would be forgotten, would disappear like the ashes dispersed to the wind from the crematoria chimneys at Auschwitz and the other extermination camps.

Ten years after the release of *Schindler's List* our knowledge is wider, but is it deeper? What has *Schindler's List* taught us? Certainly, Spielberg has said that the movie shows how one person can make a difference. But that speaks to the good in man. What does Schindler teach us about evil?

As concerns the Shoah, itself, the search for meaning must remain elusive. The words of Pinhas Epstein, a survivor of Treblinka, still ring in my ears: "Whoever was in Treblinka, will not go out of it, and whoever was not in Treblinka, will not go into Treblinka." The Holocaust is not a thing to be understood. It is an event to be remembered. It can serve as inspiration, as lesson, as reminder, as a spur—but even the survivors themselves who experienced it are at a loss to understand it.

Even more difficult, we must ask some tough questions: What good has it done to have released *Schindler's List* all over the globe in the last decade? To what end?

Was *Schindler's List* shown in Pakistan? It certainly seemed to make no impression on the murderers of Daniel Pearl who chose to film his violent death, even as they made him exclaim with his last breath, "I am a Jew." Nor has it inhibited murders in the last decade in Rwanda or currently in the Sudan—or caused the world to stop these murders.

Has it promoted tolerance and stemmed the tide of anti-Semitism? Doesn't look that way, not in Europe, the Middle East or Asia.

Has it put an end to Holocaust denial? Don't think so. But let's ask Mel Gibson's father what he thinks.

It is a curious coincidence that even as *Schindler's List* is released on DVD and its 10th anniversary is celebrated, the media has been headlining the subject of the power of film to foster anti-Semitism rather than extinguish it. *The Passion* is the 800-pound elephant in the room. No one brings it up in public, but when I mention the 10th anniversary of *Schindler* to friends, they bring up *The Passion.* As if *The Passion* is payback or backlash for years of Holocaust films. As if *The Passion* were saying: "You've had your turn making important Holocaust films, now I want to tell you the most important story for Christians—one as horrific and violent as anything that occurred during World War II. A story that the world needs to hear, know and see. A story that many people, to this day, denied occurred." As if *The Passion* is not so much anti-Semitic as it is pro-Christian, and anti-Jewish. *The Passion,* you see, is not a film about the Christ killers. Instead, it is a film that responds to the Christ deniers. Because that's who the Jews are: The people who deny that Christ is the messiah. Crazy? Sure. That's why I write "As if." But it does bring me back to my point: What 10 years later is the impact of *Schindler's List*?

To answer that question, I watched *Schindler's List* again, this time on DVD. I was more aware of the film's artistry this time—which Insdorf details with great precision in her book. What Schindler accomplished did not seem possible:

women arrived at Auschwitz, were there in fact for three weeks and Schindler was able to rescue them. It was true but never did fact seem more like fiction.

Finally, I was struck by the moral universe presented in *Schindler's List.* In Schindler we are presented with absolute evil—embodied in Amon Goeth and witnessed by the liquidation of the Krakow ghetto; and absolute good—in the words of Itzhak Stern, "The list is life." In between the two is a world of moral ambiguity.

Sid Sheinberg, the former MCA executive who first brought the novel *Schindler's List* to Spielberg's attention, told me this week that for him the essential drama of the movie is simply: "Why did he do it?" Schindler, a Nazi Party member and war profiteer, loves wine, women and fine food. He appears to be amoral in every way.

Then I recalled a peculiarity of Jewish belief—the yetzer ha'rah, or evil inclination. As Rabbi Joseph Telushkin explains in *Jewish Literacy,* Jewish tradition would have us born with the evil impulse, while the impulse to be good and altruistic, the yetzer ha'tov is thought to be a learned trait." As Jewish lore reminds us on several occasions, the evil impulse (ego, envy, lust) has often fueled great accomplishments, even good deeds. This is the story of *Schindler's List,* I realized: How greed, wine, women, lies and bribes saved Jewish lives. Schindler saved Jews by appealing to people's basest impulses.

It now appears that we were wrong to think that a movie, even one as powerful as *Schindler's List,* would rid us of Holocaust deniers, or even reduce anti-Semitism. That is not the way the world works. The evil impulse is always among us. However, we must never forget that one Schindler can subvert the evil inclination, and induce people to accomplish great things. That is man's challenge and our never-ending struggle. And, 10 years later, the lesson of *Schindler's List*.

March 12, 2004

A Sunny Hungarian Rhapsody

As winter chill gives way to spring sun, it's not too early to start planning a summer trip to Budapest.

Budapest, Hungary's capital, straddles the Danube, with historic old Buda on the hill, and Pest with its atmospheric 19th century and Art Nouveau architecture. In recent years, many of Budapest's historic sites have been restored, such as the Parliament building and St. Stephen's Church, and their interiors are breathtaking.

Part of Budapest's appeal is that it is very much a city. There's a beat, a pulse. You can head out the door; down the streets. On every corner there's something to see: There's the pedestrian mall of Vaci Utca and the enclosed Central Market with its busy stalls of foods and handicrafts. You can hop on the subway, which is easy to use and get just about anywhere. Anywhere that the trains don't go, there's a tramway waiting to take you there. Taxis abound and they are reasonable (by American standards). Budapest is small enough to get around but large enough to feel like a metropolitan cosmopolis. Many people speak English and the chirping sound of Hungarian will tickle your ears.

Budapest is also famous for its thermal hot springs and its spas, some dating back to the Roman and Ottoman empires.

The Gellert Hotel, with its renowned Turkish bath, is a delightful way to spend an afternoon and a perfect way to get over jet lag. The outdoor pool of the Gellert is also famous for its artificial waves that cascade through the pool for 10 minutes every hour and delight adults and children of all ages.

Easy walking distance from the city center is what tour books refer to as "the Jewish triangle," an area that comprises many sites of Jewish interest. There is the magnificent Dohany Synagogue, with its neo-Moorish architecture, restored to its former glory by funds from the Hungarian government and American charities. Next door is a Jewish museum housed on the site where Theodore Herzl once lived. Behind the synagogue is a Holocaust memorial sculpture. The old Jewish Quarter, where the ghetto existed under the Nazis, is there in addition to the Rumbach and Kazinczy synagogues, which are currently being renovated. A Holocaust museum is being dedicated this April, on the 50th anniversary of the Nazi's entering Budapest. Not far away is "The Terror House," a former prison that is now a museum devoted to the history and crimes of the Hungarian fascist and communist totalitarian regimes.

A visit to Budapest is also a great way to explore one's roots. The Budapest Jewish Community Center at 12 Sip Utca (street) houses record offices of the Jewish community where it is possible to locate birth, marriage and death certificates of relatives. And, if you have a date of death, you may also be able to find the graves of your relatives. In my own case I was also able to find and visit the graves of my great-uncle Hugo Hatschek (my grandmother's older brother), as well as the grave of my great-great-grandmother, Jeannette Back, who was born in 1849 and died in Budapest in 1891.

Relatives or not, I can say that one of the highlights of my trip was the almost three hours I spent early one Monday morning wandering around the Salgotarjani Utca cemetery. Opened in 1874, this is the cemetery of the Hungarian Jewish bourgeoisie. As a place to wander, this cemetery is comparable to Pere-Lachaise in Paris or Hillside in Los Angeles, for that matter.

In Salgotarjani, the walls closest to the entrance and next to the cemetery walls house the vast mausoleums of the wealthy families. They are elaborate architectural statements. In keeping with ancient Jewish tradition, the brush there grows wild. Hiking through the brambles it is possible to leave the path behind and feel lost in the necropolis. A haunting feeling: lost in the lost world of Hungarian Jewry.

As I wandered around, it was fascinating to see the names on the gravestones, itself a chronicle of assimilation. There was a vogue, apparently, for French names, as witnessed by graves of women with such unlikely Jewish names as Nannette and Babbette. Other popular Jewish names included Jospehina, Antonia and Terez (as in the empress Marie-Therese). Men's names such as Mor (Maurice) Sandor (Alexander), Vilmos, Lipot, Fulop (Phillip) are not names we think of today as Jewish but they were common then.

Budapest boasts many summer festivals, including an opera and ballet festival (August 1-19), as well as a Jewish arts festival, now in its seventh year, which will be held August 29-September 4.

Having attended last year's Jewish arts festival as a guest of the Hungarian Tourist Board, I can give you some idea of what to expect.

During the day, one is free to explore Budapest and its environs. A Jewish book festival takes place that same week—this is a festival of books in Hungarian of Jewish interest, not books in English. However it is worth stopping by, not only because they have various klezmer bands playing, but it is fascinating to see and meet young Jewish book editors, magazine owners and see the crowds of young Hungarians there for whom being Jewish is not a political act, but rather just a fact of their being—which to most Hungarians is progress.

In the evenings, there were concerts of classical music, opera, operetta as well as jazz and klezmer. There were also dance performances, even Israeli film screenings. While I was there I attended an evening of Hungarian operetta. (I have always had a weakness for Lehar's *Merry Widow.*) There was a classical music concert in the Dohany, and a performance in the State Opera House by David D'or (whom I was assured is the Israeli John Mellencamp but who seemed more like Billy Joel to me), and Dudu Fisher .

As for lodging, we were put up at the Hotel Mercur-Korona, which was located within walking distance of the Central Market, the Vaci Utca pedestrian mall and the Dohany Synagogue. The rooms were somewhat dorm-room/Ikea but I would not complain (if my wife were there, she might have). The staff were extremely helpful and the breakfasts excellent (a buffet of Hungarian cheeses, meats, vegetables, along with the usual eggs, etc.). The chain is owned by Accor, who own Motel Six in the States, and I would say it's better than that. As for other hotels, if you want the high-end, there is the Kempinski Hotel in the center of town, and the Hilton, which sits atop Buda near the old castle hill. For many years the favorite for businessmen was the Forum but it seems in need of renovation. There are also several boutique hotels that have opened in the last few years worth exploring.

But all that running around is just an excuse to kill time between meals. Leave Dr. Atkins and your diet back home. In Budapest there is not just foie gras (cold), or foie gras (hot) for which the Hungarians are justifiably famous, but let's talk goose fat, or worse yet, goose cracklings. But those were just the appetizers. By the time dessert rolled around, chestnut puree seemed like just another several-thousand calories to charm the palate with. Although I didn't make it on this trip to the tourist mecca Gundel's or to any of the classic restaurants like Apostolok (though I visited it and it looks great), Szas Eves or Matyas Pince—which I have visited on past trips. Several hip restaurants have opened such as Spoon on a barge on the Danube and the romantic Robinson's.

On my last trip, we went to a good assortment of restaurants: Jiraffe where, as an aficionado of cold cherry soup, I had a delicious cold raspberry soup; Karpathia where I gnawed on the roast goose as the zymbalom player performed my request: *The Third Man* theme. There's now a high-end restaurant at Gerbeaud's, probably the best cooking we had, but at lunch we were the only patrons (the dessert—a somloy galuska, a pound cake with cream and chocolate sauce—was off the charts). Strangely enough, one of the best meals we had was at a restaurant called Shakespeare—not the most Hungarian-sounding—but then again, Budapest boasts a statue to Shakespeare. (In fact, my grandmother's claim to fame was playing Puck in *A Midsummer's Night Dream* in

Hungarian.) So despite the name, I recommend the food at Shakespeare as delicious.

I'm getting hungry again. I may just have to go over to the Csardas restaurant on Melrose for a little a wiener schnitzel and some cucumber salad to hold me until I can get back to Budapest. Or maybe some dumpling soup and the roast duck. A little Tokay wine would be nice....

March 19, 2004

Sleep, Interrupted

I remember, as a child, trying in vain to stay up to see the ball fall on New Year's Eve. In later years, high school brought concerts that went past midnight and college introduced all-nighters of the studying and partying kind. In the midnight hour came inspiration and revelation and dreams of new worlds to conquer. Back then, sleep was not an issue.

Then sometime in my twenties, I suffered a bout of insomnia. For several weeks, I could not, did not, sleep. I can't remember why, but the gnawing numbness of that sleep deprivation—too tired to think, too awake to sleep—did not go away. Before then, sleep didn't matter; since then, I watch carefully over my sleep.

Turns out I was just a little ahead of the curve. As I passed into my thirties, it seemed everyone was concerned about sleep. In this age of 24/7, it was as if sleep had become a commodity, and there'd been a run on the product. When did sleep become "the new sex"—something everyone talks about, thinks about, but few ever have enough of?

As a married father with a mortgage and an aging prostate, there are still many nights when I wake and can't seem to fall back asleep. But I no longer lie in bed, eyes wide open, anxious, mind going a million miles an hour—or worry about how little sleep I'm getting, or if I will fall back asleep. Yes, brothers and sisters, I am here to tell you that Herr Doktor Teicholz has a cure and he is going to share it with you.

My secret is simple: If I can't sleep, I get out of bed. Most researchers agree: The bed is where you sleep, and if your eyes pop open—in the words of the Rolling Stones, "You gotta move" to another room or just another piece of furniture.

Experts also recommend that, like Lot, you avert your eyes—from finding out what time it is. My daughter wonders why we have so few clocks in the house; it's because I keep them out of my nighttime sight line.

Here's the important part: Once resettled, don't turn on the TV, which seems to stimulate the brain, rather than quiet it. I recommend reading. But not just anything.

My criteria is something that will hold your attention, divert you from your problems, but that you can pick up and put down with impunity. Although I most often read fiction for pleasure, my middle-of-the night regimen calls for nonfiction. Reading your Visa bills is a bad idea. Reading history can be a good one.

Over the years, I've found several books for midnight ramblers that fit the prescription perfectly. I will always be indebted to *Son of the Morning Star,* Evan Connell's masterfully written account of Gen. Custer and the battle of Little Bighorn for getting me through many a night, or early morning as the case may be. Connell is most known for his novels "Mr. Bridge" and "Mrs. Bridge," perhaps the finest chronicle of the interior lives of a marriage in American literature, but it his nonfiction work, *Son of the Morning Star,* that has magical properties.

It is a fascinating, extremely well-written account of something I would never have imagined would absorb me. Ten minutes of reading, and I was ready to go back to bed. Yet each time I picked up the book again, I did so with pleasure. In fact, I was sad when the book ended—and a little panicked: What would I read next?

For a while, I tried biographies. Teddy Roosevelt, Churchill, whatever was gathering dust on the living room coffee table. Didn't work for me.

The problem with biographies is that the first half is all good news—there are hardships and travails, but they are inevitably overcome. It was the second half that I had a problem with—disappointment, decline, illness and death—such is the rub in life itself and being reminded of it at four a.m. is no plus.

By contrast, I've had great success with Joseph Telushkin's *Jewish Literacy*. Close readers of this column will know that I often reference the work when I want to pass for Torah savvy or Tanakh fabulous.

Mostly, though, I dip into it at night. The book is more than 700 pages long and there are 348 entries, each a few pages long. At that time of night, my powers of retention vary, and so sometimes I read sections I don't realize I've read before; sometimes I read them again because I don't remember them; and sometimes I have great realizations reading them, which I often forget upon waking. But it never fails to capture my imagination and then lead me back to bed.

Most recently, I've started in on Edith Grossman's new translation of Cervantes' *Don Quixote*. The knight errant of Galicia quickly transports me away from twenty-first century concerns.

The book is surprisingly sly, deft and comic—a virtuoso fifteenth century metanovel. And the chapters are short—always a plus in matters of sleep hygiene.

I'm only 200 pages in and will report at some future date on the full Mancha, but for now, suffice to say, Grossman's wonderful rendering makes returning to my dreams, possible.

We live in a culture (and a city) where people strive for self-improvement. They work out, they obsess about their appearance (and improve it beyond God's gifts). They seek to look better and live longer.

At the same time, they neglect sleep, to which we devote one-third of our lives. That, I would argue is a mistake. Instead, they should do a little night reading to improve their lives.

March 26, 2004

Second Government

Bernard-Henri Levy

I've been thinking a lot recently about French philosopher, journalist and filmmaker Bernard-Henri Levy (only in France can philosopher hyphenate with filmmaker).

We had lunch about six months ago. At the time, Levy's English-language edition of *Who Killed Daniel Pearl?* (Melville House), had just been published. The book had received a mixed response for its controversial thesis that Daniel Pearl was murdered because he was on the trail of a larger story, of connections between Pakistani security forces, Pakistan's nuclear establishment and Al Qaeda.

Levy felt that Pearl's murder was "a hinge" moment in modern history. He had spent a year retracing Pearl's steps, reliving and re-imagining his last moments. It was, he said, "the strangest adventure that has ever happened to me."

Levy's book served an important agenda: to make the death of Pearl a subject of discussion and scrutiny, of international importance both as a murder demanding justice and as an international incident with nefarious implications worth investigating.

Today, more than two years since Pearl's murder, the four men convicted of the death in Pakistan await their appeal, and four others who were detained in connection with the crime have yet to be charged.

Nonetheless, since Levy's book, Pakistani nuclear scientist Abdul Qadeer Khan has confessed to fifteen years of sharing Pakistan's nuclear secrets with Iran, North Korea and Libya, vindicating Levy's claims. However, Pakistan President Pervez Musharaf, after a private interview, the substance of which has never been made public, pardoned Khan.

Recently, another book of Levy's, *War, Evil and the End of History* (Melville House), was published in English. From May 30 to June 4, 2001, at the behest of the French newspaper, Le Monde, Levy traveled to five of the world's unheralded hot spots: Sri Lanka, Burundi, Colombia, Sudan and Angola. His first-person accounts of "forgotten wars" are chilling.

Levy's goal is simple: to wake us up to human suffering and injustice at a time when Israel and Iraq seem to occupy all the intellectual, emotional and journalistic real estate. We need this now more than ever.

There is a great line in *Control Room,* the documentary about the Al Jazeera network, when Hassan Ibrahim, one of their reporters, remarks, "See, the problem with the Middle East is that everything is an Israeli conspiracy—everything. If a water pipe breaks in the center of Damascus, it will be blamed on the Israelis, instead of blaming it on our incompetence."

Levy asks us not to forget that globalization means that we are charged with bringing the entire world to account, not just those we wish to politicize, demonize or sentimentalize. We must not, Levy writes "be seduced into finding meaning where none exists." In terms of philosophy, he pits Walter Benjamin against Hegel or "dry indignant anger against the consolation of dialetics."

In Sri Lanka, Levy interviews a woman trained to be a suicide bomber—or as Levy calls them, kamikazes. In Colombia, he meets with government officials, revolutionary leaders (so-called) and coca farmers. In the Sudan, where over the last several years a genocide of Christians has been occurring, he explores the role of oil in the Sudan's vale of destruction.

Perhaps it's a coincidence that Secretary of State Colin Powell has in the last few weeks traveled to a refugee camp in the Sudan and the United Nations has started to threaten sanctions. Consider Levy's call to arms part of the tipping point that made it such that the world could no longer look the other way.

Alexander Solzhenitsyn once opined that writers should be like "a second government." Back when this country was young, Tom Paine wrote that "my country is the world, and my religion is to do good." In the 1960s, Norman Mailer, Gore Vidal, Kurt Vonnegut and William F. Buckley were all part of the national debate. But in truth, it's been a while since we've had men of letters rising to the level of conscience of the nation.

Today, we've passed into an age of punditry. Our opinion makers are for the most part entertainers—Rush Limbaugh, the Fox crew, Al Franken, Howard Stern. Add multimillionaire populist Michael Moore to the list.

No one can argue with the phenomenal success of *Fahrenheit 9/11*. By now, even the most serious of columnists, Tom

Freidman, William Safire and Andrew Sullivan, are humming MC Hammer's refrain, "Can't touch this."

This makes a certain amount of sense, given that, as noted in an NEA study released this month, people are reading less. Even our president has admitted that he doesn't read the news.

Conversely, this makes writers like Levy all the more important. Despite our 24/7 TV news channels, the always-on Internet, as well as daily local and national newspapers, the biggest news stories of recent months have appeared in books—Paul O'Neal's, Richard Clarke's, Bob Woodward's. Talk about old school. At the same time, some of the best reporting about the war in Iraq, including the Abu Gharib prisoner abuse scandal, have been reported by veteran journalist Seymour Hersh in The New Yorker magazine—yes, The New Yorker—leaving the newspapers and major networks to spin the information—commenting rather than breaking the news.

History will repeat itself, if we choose to ignore it. Let me leave the last word to Levy who writes: "We'll have to do what the American soldiers did in 1944 after the liberation of the camps, when they forced the German city dwellers to file past the corpses. Innocent, the ordinary German citizens? Never, ever lent a hand to the crematoriums of Bergen-Belsen? Maybe. If you like. But that's not the question now. The gesture, all the same, of the Americans forcing them just to file by, to look, to keep their eyes open, above all not to go back to sleep. A good metaphor, in short, for the role of intellectuals."

March 28, 2004

The Escapist

Michael Chabon's *The Escapist* as metaphor

It's Sunday and I'm rushing over to my local comic book store, Hi De Ho, in Santa Monica to buy issue No. 1 of *The Amazing Adventures of the Escapist.*

If the name is familiar, it's not because you used to collect *The Escapist* in your youth, as many people have told Mike Hennessy, the owner of Hi De Ho. Rather *The Escapist* is a fictional invention—I know that seems evident, but what I mean is that *The Escapist* first appeared in text form in Michael Chabon's Pulitzer prize-winning novel, *The Amazing Adventures of Kavalier and Clay* as the comic book that his protagonists created.

So many readers believed in *The Escapist,* a hero who is part Houdini and part Batman, and Chabon fell so under the spell of his own fictional creation, that he has agreed to continue the fiction into comic book form. *The Escapist* comic book pretends to reprint past *Escapist* stories.

Mike Richardson of Dark Horse Comics has enabled Chabon, as well as comic book regulars Howard Chaykin and Kevin McCarthy, to contribute to the mythology of this singular hero, who comes "to the aid of all those who languish in tyranny's chains!"

A great part of the charm of *Kavalier and Clay*, as well as this new comic book incarnation, resides in the metaphor of *The Escapist*. In the novel, Joseph Kavalier, a Czech Holocaust refugee, draws a comic hero who delivers a powerful response to evil, even as Kavalier himself remains powerless to help his relatives escape their fate in Europe.

Escape is a potent concept, and Chabon is certainly not the first to seize on it. Houdini turned escape into a performance art. For a fascinating meditation on the psychological and philosophical implications of Houdini's life and art, I can recommend no better work than British analyst Adam Phillips' *Houdini's Box: The Art of Escape*.

As Phillips relates, Houdini was born Erik Weisz in Budapest in 1874, and he escaped his name, his traditions and poverty by being a master of illusion—his first famous trick was called, appropriately enough, "metamorphosis." Part of Houdini's appeal was that he appeared to escape death in his performances. That, as Houdini came to believe, is something people will always pay money to see. It is a lesson that is not lost on David Blaine (a performer who has tattooed Primo Levi's Auschwitz number on his arm—as if to link one escape artist to another).

The Escapist references not only the primal appeal of escapism but also comics as a medium suited for Jewish metamorphosis. It is commonly accepted that Superman, created by Jerry Siegel and Joe Shuster in the 1930s, was a metaphor for Jewish identity, assimilation, weakness and power—whether they knew it at the time or not.

But I would argue that the tale of the escapist is part of our mythological DNA, deeply ingrained in our most sacred stories.

Perhaps it's no coincidence that I first read Bible stories in comic book form.

Metamorphosis and escape are core themes in the Pentateuach. Adam and Eve were certainly the first escapists, and Big Daddy Abraham, patriarch of patriarchs, was the first Jewish escapist, commanded to leave his father's home. Jacob, Job, Joseph—the list of escapists goes on and on.

This week we celebrate perhaps the greatest Jewish escapist: Moses. As a baby Moses escaped into the bulrushes; as a young man, he escaped after murdering an Egyptian overseer; and, of course, he led the escape from Egypt. Moses makes Kafka look like a one-trick pony: Moses changes into an Egyptian noble, into a desert herder—and from a stutterer to a leader. He's got more changes than David Bowie.

One could recast all of Jewish history as a series of escapes, from Egypt, Babylonia, Spain, England, Russia—an epic Purimspiel. However to do so would diminish Jewish history to a repeating loop of persecution and escape that begs the question: Is the Holocaust the story of the murder of 6 million, or the survival of 6 million? A history of escapes leaves out the glory of the art of *The Escapist*—and the richness of Jewish culture.

As Houdini understood so well, escape is great entertainment—particularly for those who are not the ones escaping. Artists have been providing escapism as entertainment since stories were first told. Even today, in America, Land of the Free, where we need not escape, we still enjoy being armchair escapists. Is it a coincidence that one of the most popular shows on television is called *Survivor*?

The history of comic books, like that of the motion picture business, has been driven by Jewish escape artists, from the 1940s and the golden age of Siegel and Shuster to the early 1960s and Stan Lee, whose Fantastic Four and other Marvel comics reinvigorated the genre, to Robert Crumb, who took the comix, as he called them, into the underground, and also to Will Eisner, whose 1978 *A Contract With God* launched the graphic novel.

Over the next decade, as movies, TV and video games came to dominate the culture, comic books seemed to diminish in importance. By the end of the 1980s, comics seemed played out, in need of a superhero to save the day. It wasn't a bird or a plane, but rather a *Maus.*

Art Speigelman's "survivor's tale" made the comic book worthy, winning the 1992 Pulitzer Prize and demonstrating that graphic novels were an independent medium for telling personal stories. Since *Maus,* a whole shelf of important and provocative works has appeared, including such diverse works as Alan Moore's *Watchmen,* Joe Kubert's F*ax From Sarajevo* and Marjane Satrapi's *Persepolis: The Story of a Childhood.*

Which brings me back to Hi De Ho. When I was a kid, comic books were mostly sold in candy stores. When those disappeared, they moved to newsstands and supermarkets. Today, stores like Hi De Ho sell more comics in book form than magazine format.

For a while, comics were primarily the obsession of young kids, then just teenage boys, then just collectors. Today, comic books and comic book stores are much more female friendly. As Hennessy told me, "Once they [comics] were no longer about guys in tights beating on each other" women became interested. The variety of work is amazing: Japanese, European, gothic, fantastic and classic. There are now comics for every age and every interest, from the prurient to the depraved.

Comics, which had abandoned young readers for several decades, are catering to them once again. Archie and Veronica are still around, but they have competition from *The Simpsons*. Disney, which has always produced popular children's comic books in Europe, has returned to the American market.

My daughter, who is just starting to read, was so excited when I brought home her own first comic, the new issue of *Duck Tales*. As she scanned the cartoon panels, making up her own story to fill what she could not yet understand, I saw a look in her eye, one that I recalled from my own youth. It was the look of an "escapist."

April 9, 2004

The End of *Friends*

The last episode of *Friends* airs May 6, and while we may all express a collective sigh of relief at the end of more than a year of shameless hype and exploitation, it doesn't mean that we can't stop to reflect on this moment in American cultural history. Or that we don't care about whether Ross and Rachel will get together.

One may debate whether Marta Kauffman and David Crane's *Friends* will join the ranks of comedy classics, but it was a show that had many, many great comic moments, a cast that played so well off each other and writers who were able to reap maximum humor from the talents and personalities of their six main actors. Rewatching the pilot episode recently, it was all there from the beginning—the chemistry between the actors, and the quick quips and repartee in the writing.

No matter how artificial the construct of a sitcom, from the start *Friends* stood out and was buoyed by the essential truth it explored: that there's a period of time in our lives—post-college, at first jobs, figuring out life, love, adulthood—when our friends become our family.

Friends leaves us at a time of particular weakness for the sitcom as several other classics are also fading. *Frasier,* which managed to channel Jack Benny and Georges Feydeau in equal parts, is ending this year. I will miss it. *Everybody Loves Raymond* is leaving next year after a truncated season. My sadness is also personal: *Frasier* and *Raymond* are the last in a long line of shows I enjoyed and discussed with my mother, a connoisseur of the sitcom who died three and a half years ago. As a child, my mother thought it more important that I watch *Lucy* or old *Burns and Allen* shows than do my homework (which explains a lot about my life).

The sitcom is also losing ground to unscripted shows—so-called reality TV. In truth, *Friends* seems very much of an era—the optimistic and lighthearted 1990s, the self-obsessed years of the Internet bubble. Today everything has become more serious. Ironically right after September 11 many pundits opined that America would turn to comedy and traditional sitcoms for comfort—it turns out they were wrong. In order to avoid reality, we demand not sitcoms but "reality TV." As Jeff Zucker, el presidente of NBC Entertainment, recently told The New York Times, "turns out the next *Friends* was not a half-hour scripted comedy. It was *The Apprentice*."

Perhaps, in a world of uncertainty, sitcoms are too scripted. So we have found alternatives to our reality in unscripted, but nonetheless unreal programming. At a time when people are struggling to find a job, and where the millions of Americans who've lost their jobs are bravely living day by day, we watch people vie to start at the top, and thrill to hear Donald Trump, certainly the least authentic person in America, say, "You're fired." Instead of sitcoms, where unlikely groups of people share apartments and fall in love, we are watching *The Bachelor, The Bachelorette* and *Average Joe,* all competitions for a diamond ring, not a brass one.

Talk about holding up a mirror to our times: rather than

acknowledge the reality of how we look in America—in a country that has both an epidemic of obesity and record cases of anorexia—we are compelled by *Extreme Makeover* and *The Swan,* where happiness is achieved at knife point. We prefer our reality to have a happy ending, or at least a meaningful one. We debate showing the corpses flayed in Fallujah, as we go in record numbers to watch the graphic flaying in *The Passion of the Christ.* These are the times we live in, where we flock to manufactured versions of reality. Given the reality, I can't blame them.

If I am sad at all about the end of *Friends* after 236 episodes, it's because the show poses a question that is also true to life: Does the end of *Friends* mean the end of friends?

Monica and Chandler are moving to the suburbs and adopting a child. Joey is moving to Los Angeles to pursue his acting career. Phoebe is married as well. As for Ross and Rachel their future is uncertain. We wonder for them, as we do for David Schwimmer, Jennifer Aniston and the rest of the cast: Will they able to keep the friends they made over the last decade? Will they make new ones? Will we?

Children play with anyone—they are delighted to make new friends. In our twenties, we also make new friends, friends who are our companions as we make fools of ourselves in a thousand ways, as we explore living apart from our parents, making our first homes, finding love in places wrong and/or with Mr. or Ms. Right. But then as we move on to new jobs, new homes and/or committed relationships with or without children, we seem to lose those friends. How often have people looked at their wedding albums to comment about how few of the people in the pictures they still know.

The importance of *Friends* may be argued, but the importance of friendship cannot be overrated. On an occasion such as this, it would be hard to resist quoting Cicero, who said of friendship that "with the exception of wisdom, no better thing has been given to man by the immortal gods."

April 30, 2004

Breaking the Mold

Eric Lax's book on the discovery of penicillin

Earlier this month I attended the Juvenile Diabetes Research Foundation research benefit for stem-cell research. Although James Taylor's five-song set and Nancy Reagan's acceptance speech were each memorable and moving, what I found myself thinking about most that evening was Eric Lax's new book *The Mold in Dr. Florey's Coat* (Henry Holt & Company, twenty-five dollars), about the story of penicillin.

In the sixty years since it was first made available, penicillin has gone from miracle drug, to cure-all, to over-prescribed. Today it's common to hear Westside mothers brag about not using antibiotics. Lax, however, takes us back to a time when a simple infection could lead unexpectedly to death. Doctors for the most part, followed the oath to do no harm, but they could do little proactively to reverse the course of a serious infection.

As described by Lax, the history of penicillin was something of a relay race. Microbiologist Alexander Fleming was the first to explore the special properties of this distinctive mold in his London lab in 1928. However, by 1932 Fleming had abandoned his research, because he saw no way to extract the penicillin. Almost a decade later, Howard Florey had assembled a team of scientists to research antibiotic agents when biochemist Ernst Chain, a German Jewish refugee who had arrived in London in 1933 with ten pounds sterling in his pocket, came upon Fleming's original paper. Chain, along with Edward Abraham, was able to solve the mystery of penicillin's chemical nature. Norman Heatley and Gordon Saunders, for their part, invented homemade solutions for extracting and purifying penicillin from the molds.

Even so, the British discoveries would not, by themselves, have made penicillin the World War II lifesaver it became. Of critical importance, American pharmaceutical companies came up with a more potent variant of penicillin (from a cantaloupe) and ways to increase the amount that could be fermented (think vats of beer). In 1941, Florey could only produce enough penicillin to conduct several tests. By 1944, the United States was producing 100 billion units per month, saving hundreds of thousands of soldiers and civilians.

Lax uncovers the human drama behind the story: Fleming's reticent nature, which at first worked against him and finally made him credible in the role of "the modest man of science"; Florey's constant struggle to fund his research, his loveless marriage, as well as his twenty-five year affair with his colleague Margaret Jennings, whom he married after his wife's death in 1966; and Heatley's war-time romance in Iowa. At the same time, we see Chain's voluble personality and his encounters with British anti-Semitism. This is made all the more dramatic against a backdrop of war—The Battle of Britain, and the Blitz (the book's title comes from Florey's suggestion that if the Nazis capture them they should destroy their work but keep the penicillin mold alive in the pockets of their coat). At the same time, Lax chronicles how the story of penicillin took on a life of its own.

Popular accounts gave Fleming all the credit for "discovering" penicillin, although he basically abandoned his research early on. Florey and Chain shared the Nobel Prize with Fleming, and received much professional distinction for their work, but Heatley got very little. The British regarded taking a patent on the process as something that was "not done." American pharmaceutical companies (Merck, Abbott and Pfizer) felt differently and reaped tremendous royalties. Lax's tome sets the record straight and gives the right persons their due—all in a very readable fashion. As several reviewers have already noted, Lax has taken his talents as a biographer of famous actors (Woody Allen, Humphrey Bogart) and his abilities as a science writer (*Life and Death on 10 West*) and brought them to bear on Fleming, Florey, Chain, et al.

For Los Angeles author Lax, whom I know from the writer's human rights organization PEN USA (he's copresident and a board member of PEN International), the book represents a five-year journey that began when he read the obituary of Anne Miller in 1999, a woman who, in 1942, was among the first to be brought back from certain death by penicillin. Lax is intelligent, charming and has a certain intensity—the book is very much like him. Although much of the story takes place in England, it makes perfect sense that writing it would appeal to someone from Los Angeles.

More than anything else, Lax's book conveys the sanguine worldview that drove disparate characters to succeed in one of the greatest medical discoveries of our times. This cannot be understated.

Lax came to Los Angeles in 1980 to write an article for New West magazine. The assignment, about the bone marrow transplantation ward at UCLA, turned into the book *Life and Death on 10 West.* Lax stayed on and, as a nonfiction writer in a town of screenwriters, he has been fortunate to make a life here with his wife and two sons. I don't think it's a coincidence that a former Peace Corps worker moves to California, has the impact he has had with PEN and now writes a book about "the penicillin miracle." Los Angeles is a place of enormous optimism, a city driven on hope.

Which brings me back to the Juvenile Diabetes stem-cell research benefit: Much as we may take antibiotics for granted, we still stand powerless before a host of debilitating and fatal diseases, such as Alzheimer's, ALS, Parkinson's and diabetes. Lax's book is a timely and powerful reminder that investing in science and research can be a matter of life or death.

May 21, 2004

Most of the Best

S. J. Perelman

Among the allergens being released this June is a remake of *Around the World in 80 Days,* the Jules Verne novel that launched a thousand travel articles. Perhaps Jackie Chan will inhabit the role of Passepartout in a fashion that surpasses the achievements of Cantinflas, "the world's greatest comedian," according to Charlie Chaplin, a person of no small ego or talent himself. That remains to be seen—or not seen, as the case may be.

Although this remake gives license to recall the 1956 Mike Todd extravaganza, my purpose is slightly different: I want to pay tribute to the man who won an Oscar for doing punch-up on that screenplay—none other than that nonpareil, S.J. Perelman.

This year is the 100th anniversary of the birth of Sydney Joseph Perelman ("Sid" to his friends, Mr. Perelman to me). I have been awaiting the coast-to-coast and worldwide celebrations, the star-studded readings, film festivals and parties—the free food and booze to which all writers consecrate their art, but thus far, the silence has been deafening.

Perelman, who died in 1979, is little remembered today. Many of his works are out of print, and his films (with the exception of his work for the Brothers Marx) little seen. In 2000, the Modern Library issued an abridged collection of his greatest hits, *Most of the Most of S. J. Perelman.*

Steve Martin's name appears on the cover for no apparent reason other than to convey hipness by association. It is my hope that as long as people need to laugh, Perelman will be read.

Although Perelman called himself a "miniaturist," he published twenty-two books, including collections of his short "embroidery," as well as book-length travel books, such as *Westward Ha!* and *The Swiss Family Perelman.* He also wrote more than ten produced screenplays and seven plays. Asked what the inspiration was for this prodigious output, Perelman replied: "The landlord."

During his lifetime, Perelman made six circumnavigations of the globe, driven not so much by wanderlust as the realization that inclement conditions often brought out the best in his writing. Or as Perelman put it so succinctly, "Misery breeds copy."

Perelman was born in Brooklyn, raised in Providence and matriculated from Brown University, where he was editor of The Brown Jug, the college humor magazine. Upon graduation, he started out as a cartoonist but quickly turned to the short form for which he would become famous. A brief stint writing for Judge, a humor magazine, was notable for Perelman meeting its editor, Harold Ross, who would publish Perelman at his next magazine, *The New Yorker.*

Perelman saw himself as working in a tradition of comic writing: He followed Stephen Leacock and George Ade, names long lost to us, and emulated Ring Lardner and H.L. Mencken. The mixture of Brooklyn and Brown gave Perelman both the education and the vantage point to observe, record and deflate pretension wherever he found it—he could look down with equal aplomb at Hollywood moguls, intellectuals and/or society swells.

The Marx Brothers brought Perelman to Hollywood to write *Horsefeathers* and *Monkey Business.* Shortly thereafter, he and his wife, Laura, became contract writers at MGM under Irving Thalberg, writing scripts for now forgotten films with such fragrant titles as *Sitting Pretty, Ambush!* and *Boy Trouble.*

Perelman spent much of the 1930s in Hollywood, and over the years it was a subject he attacked with splenetic glee—of which we continue to be the beneficiaries.

"During that epoch, I made my living for the silver screen," Perelman wrote, "an occupation which, like herding swine, makes the vocabulary pungent but contributes little to one's prose style."

Or consider this billet-doux: "Hollywood is a dreary industrial town controlled by hoodlums of enormous wealth, the ethical sense of a pack of jackals and taste so degraded that it befouled everything it touched."

But tell us, Mr. Perelman, what you really think.

Perelman's work was first published in *The New Yorker* in 1930, and it continued to appear there for more than four decades. Perelman described his writing style as "a mixture of all the trash I read as a child, all the clichés, criminal slang, liberal doses of Yiddish and some of what I learned in school from impatient teachers."

Perelman dressed British and talked Yiddish, literally. An Anglophile in matters of dress and manners, he didn't seem to have much truck with the faith of his fathers. Yet Yiddish was his lingua franca; it seasoned his every conversation. Perelman achieved in this manner an assimilation that brought Perelman into the mainstream and Yiddish into American letters and culture.

If The Streets or Eminem have done nothing to reassure you about the resilience of the English language, a trip on the SS Perelman may prove salutary. What makes Perelman so enthralling, so entertaining, so inspiring to read to this very day is his ability to make every word count (even if they are of his own invention) and every other word sing like some gin-soaked chantootsie.

For readers, students of the genre and imitators such as myself, a dose of Perelman is a powerful tonic, likely to make one fall off the couch laughing. But don't take my word for it. Here's what Groucho said in a letter to Perelman: "From the moment I picked up your book until I put it down, I was convulsed with laughter. One day I intend to read it."

I recommend that you read it as well. *Most of the Most of Perelman* will certainly provide more entertainment than some of the remake of *Around the World,* hands down, sight unseen.

June 4, 2004

Playing in Uketopia

Jim Beloff and the ukelele

It's Sunday night and a half-dozen people are onstage at McCabe's Guitar Shop in Santa Monica. Jumpin' Jim Beloff and his wife, Leapin' Liz, are leading the sold-out crowd as they strum their ukuleles and sing "Farewell."

This is the climax to Uketopia, Beloff's annual celebration of that four-stringed wonder: the ukulele. It is an evening in which almost a dozen performers, from twenties to nineties, including the self-declared "Mr. Ukulele," Charles "Soybean" Sawyer, Fred Sokolow and "King Kukulele," played two-song sets each of Hawaiian, Jamaican and Tin Pan Alley tunes—everything from Sophie Tucker's "Making Wicky Wacky down in Waikiki" to a soulful rendition of Bob Marley's "Redemption Song."

When I last saw Beloff, many moons ago, he was living in New York selling advertising space for Ziff-Davis computer publications. He and Liz, his recently betrothed, were buying a loft, and I was, of all things, their real estate attorney—it was that long ago. Last I heard, Jim had moved to Los Angeles and became associate publisher of Billboard. That made sense, because even in my dim remembrance of things past Beloff was always playing music.

By 1992, although he and Liz loved Los Angeles, he was not so crazy about Billboard. It's never a good sign when your worst fear is getting promoted. In New York, he and Liz were flea market fans, so they were eager to make a pilgrimage to the Rose Bowl where, on their very first visit, Beloff came upon a Martin Tenor ukulele. His father-in-law had played one, so he picked it up. Within a week, he recalls, he became obsessed.

When Beloff found that most old ukulele songbooks were out of print, he approached Hal Leonard, the largest songbook publisher, and suggested writing a new one. At Liz's suggestion, Beloff took on the moniker "Jumpin' Jim" and the book exceeded all expectations. A how-to-play book followed. Beloff then collaborated on a visual history of the ukulele.

As Beloff tells it, it was a boatload of Portuguese workers from the island of Madeira that first brought a four-string instrument to Hawaii in 1879. I would love to tell you that they were descendants of Marranos who had fled the Inquisition, but there is no evidence of that, save their affection for sweet wine. The playing style and sound reminded the natives of U-kooley'ley, or jumping fleas. Soon the Hawaiians were making the instruments out of native wood. When the king started playing, a national craze was born. An exhibition at the Hawaiian pavilion at San Francisco's 1915 Panama Pacific exhibition launched America's romance with all things Hawaiian, lasting until the Jazz Age. The second ukulele craze came in the 1950s—many Americans serving in the South Pacific had caught "tiki fever" and when the Eisenhower era's "king of all media," Arthur Godfrey, played a plastic ukulele on his show, sales shot up by 9 million. However, a decade later the ukulele death knell sounded as "Tiny Tim" made the uke into a kitsch artifact.

The third wave of the ukulele explosion began in the early '90s as bands in Hawaii, such as the Ka'au Crater Boys, made the uke relevant to a new generation. At the same time Beloff continued to publish songbooks of showtunes, surf songs, island songs and movie music. No less a cultural seer than Leonard Maltin, a uke collector and player himself, has dubbed Beloff "the Johnny Appleseed of the uke."

In 1998, Beloff said "sayonara" (or "aloha" as the case may be) to corporate life. He and Liz started an Internet-based business called Flea Market Music that sells songbooks, CDs and instructional videos. When people kept asking, "Can you recommend a ukulele?" Beloff turned to his brother-in-law, an engineer, to come up with a made-in-America plastic ukulele, with good sound, great design, at a reasonable price. The Flea Market Music ukulele or "The Fluke" as Liz named it, appeared at a trade show in 1999. Priced at 179 dollars, including case, the orders started piling up. "The Flea" a slightly smaller and lower-priced model (149 dollars, case included) appeared a few years later, and are now sold at music stores nationwide, including McCabes and through their Web site www.fleamarketmusic.com.

One of the high points for Beloff came in 1999, when uke fan George Harrison came by his home and scribbled an appreciation on the spot. And lest you doubt that the ukulele is a full-blown phenomenon, watch the crowd go wild when Eddie Vedder starts playing his onstage.

Today, Beloff is a man who smiles a lot. He is a part of a generation of guys I know who came under the spell of James Taylor and other singer-songwriters of the 1970s. They bought guitars and strummed songs, jammed with friends, formed bands and dreamed of lives playing music. They played frat parties, bars and coffeehouses. Sunday brunch at the Four Oaks. Busking in the subways in Paris. But as they stood Robert Johnson-like at the Crossroads of their early twenties, they wondered what to do with their lives.

They were nice Jewish boys. For most, the call of professional life was stronger than the call of the road. Some became music arrangers, others music executives, managers or attorneys. Even if they left the music world, a visit to their home would always reveal that one place, the music room where they keep their guitars. And in some deep recess of their soul, reserved for the weekend, was the thought: "I have to get back to the music."

So after all these years, there's Jim up on stage, playing music and performing songs that he wrote. When he and Liz launched into a rousing rendition of Carl Sigman & Herb Magidson's, "Enjoy Yourself (It's Later Than You Think)," I had to agree. They get to play. And, it's my good fortune that I get to write about them. Ain't life grand?

June18, 2004

The Kid Still Stays in the Picture

Robert Evans

Tommywood was expecting a Hollywood moment. Publicity guru extraordinaire Michael Levine had arranged for me to meet legendary Producer Robert Evans at his longtime lair, Woodland, the former home of Greta Garbo. I turned north of Sunset Boulevard and, like William Holden, wondered what I was getting myself into.

It's not that I didn't appreciate Evans' accomplishments. Evans, the former head of production at Paramount, was responsible for *Love Story*, *The Godfather*, and *Chinatown* among many other classic films. He is the only producer to have two films on the national preservation list.

His best-selling autobiography, *The Kid Stays in the Picture,* was chosen by the Library of Congress as a required text for every branch. The audio version of *The Kid* voiced by Evans has become a cult sensation, passed from hand to hand, making Evans an idol to a new generation.

When I listened to it, I often had to pull over to stop from laughing. The book begat a very enjoyable documentary of the same name and even an animated cartoon, *Kid Notorious,* which ran on Comedy Central and which director-savant Brett Ratner has committed to turning into a feature-length animated movie.

So I had read, heard and seen Evans, past and present.

Just check out young Evans in the Lon Chaney biopic *Man of a Thousand Faces* playing MGM's Irving Thalberg. One watches agog at the surreal performance of an actor who will one day run a studio, playing a studio head. Hard to imagine that ever happening again.

I knew that many had fallen under Evans' spell. Kissinger, in his Henry the K days, camped out at Woodland. More recently, Ratner bivouacked there.

Perhaps Kissinger, like many a politician, wanted some of the Hollywood fairy dust. Perhaps Ratner was in search of a father figure, or maybe Evans had a certain sophistication he desired. But for me, at this point, Evans held little appeal, save camp curiosity.

Recently, when Evans appeared on Chris Matthew's *Hardball* to discuss the legacy of Ronald Reagan, Evans said of the former president's qualifications: "Why not an actor?"

Why not indeed, I thought as I pulled into Evans' long, narrow driveway, shaded by thick, gnarled trees that made me think of a Louisiana swamp, past a tennis court and the burned-out shell of a building (Evans' pool house had burned down, the victim of an exploding plasma screen TV). I had left the real world behind.

Once inside, I was asked to wait in the living room. There were two couches facing each other. A coffee table piled with books. A baby grand. Art on the wall: a Bernard Buffet, a Rembrandt sketch—a giant photo from the late Helmut Newton, inscribed: "To my Bobbie, the last tycoon." A Beverly Hills version of a Park Avenue apartment—the vibe was from another time, yet timeless; elegant, yet mannered. A stage set where every knickknack, every tchotchke, was perfectly placed.

Evans appeared. Although it was past two p.m., Evans was still in his bathrobe. He shuffles a bit, but he stands tall, tanned, his hair long, his glasses tinted. Considering that he suffered a triple stroke a few years ago, he looks terrific.

We sat and talked. And talked. And talked. What was supposed to be twenty minutes turned into two hours. We discussed some of his current projects—Evans still has a film deal at Paramount with "more projects than ever." He's also considering several reality series—either as subject or judge.

There's even the possibility of a one-man show, *An Evening With Robert Evans,* if you will, where between clips, he would tell anecdotes about his life and the famous lives he's known (not unlike the programs Cary Grant or Gregory Peck put together in their last years). Finally, Evans is completing his second volume of autobiography, *The Fat Lady Sang,* which begins with the stroke that doctors felt he would never survive.

What surprised me was that Evans' rap was unexpectedly deep, philosophical, even spiritual. Yes, famous names came up (Sumner Redstone, Jack Nicholson, Cagney to name a few) and famous anecdotes told, including one about dropping acid with Grant. Yes, there were allusions to Evans' many sexual conquests—a word rhyming with wussy was mentioned, the implication being that there was still no lack thereof. But those were just passing references.

Strangely enough, what Evans wanted to talk about—what

lured me to enter his bedroom and get up on his bed with him to watch a video—was, I kid you not, a film he had made about Pope John Paul II.

Let me explain: The 1980s were for Evans not unlike the 18-minute gap on Nixon/Rosemary Woods' tape—a period for which we can only imagine the worst, and that the principals wish were forgotten.

Somewhere in between the scandals, and as Evans own life careened out of control (mountains of cocaine were involved), as he lost most of what was dear to him, Evans saw a story about the pope going to meet Ali Agca Mehmet, the man who had attempted to assassinate him, to forgive him. Evans spent two million dollars of his own money making a documentary about the pope—even managed to get Donna Summer to sing with a choir on the soundtrack.

Evans had a certain insight into the holy father. "Who is the pope?" Evans asked me. "Do you know what he did before he became a priest? Before the war?"

I shrugged.

"Karol Woytila was," Evans said with a certain satisfaction, "an actor!"

Evans convinced the Vatican to allow him to use the footage of the pope meeting with Mehmet. The resulting ecumenical film, *The Planet Is Alive,* was made, Evans said, "as a present for the Pope."

The film has not been shown in this country. Although he's had offers from American networks, Evans insists the documentary be aired commercial free.

In Russia, the documentary was first shown in its entirety on Christmas Day 1991—and has been aired every Christmas since. Evans believes the documentary has contributed to the massive explosion of religious expression of all faiths, including Judaism, in the former Soviet Union.

Although Evans' parents were Jewish—they only attended services on the High Holy Days—Evans rarely went, never received religious instruction and never was bar mitzvahed. In fact, as a child actor, he was much criticized for playing a Nazi in a radio play. In later years, the closest he came to observance was hosting a Passover seder at his home, with Kirk Douglas officiating, to woo Roman Polanski to direct *Chinatown.*

In fact, Evans is quick to offer that he blames religion for pitting people against each other, rather than bringing them together. Part of what moved him so about the pope's act was that it showed the healing power of forgiveness. A power that Evans did not know he would have to call upon.

However, Evans feels that making that film is the reason that he is alive today. Why, despite the best doctors' diagnosis to the contrary, he survived his three strokes. He believes in God—not religion.

Evans screened the twenty-minute trailer for the film. Evans said that of all the films he has made, it is the one of which he is most proud.

It was incredibly compelling to see the pope walking down the prison corridor to his assassin's cell and incredibly powerful to see the pope conferring with Mehmet. I was moved.

Evans, the master seducer, had won me over. At that point, I was ready to move in and never leave Woodland. All I wanted was to hear more.

Later, I tried to figure out what had happened. For some reason, what came to mind was Bela Lugosi's Dracula. Remember the opening scene—Dracula appears in a cloak, exuding old world charm, and his voice, his home, all contrive to cast a spell. It was like that. I was hypnotized.

Perhaps, like Dracula, Evans offered in his anecdotes, in his home, the promise of a world where time stopped, where the dead lived on, where past transgressions were forgiven, where God exists to heal, where sex (or the life force) is eternal, where even the living need not die, where, like Evans, one could live beyond death itself and live to write about it.

Yes, I wanted to move in. Or at least come back next week to pitch some projects.

July 2, 2004

Rambamalama

The Rambam, Rabbi Leder, and Julie Salamon

Put down your *Da Vinci Code.* Set aside your *South Beach Diet.* Let your kaballah red string drop off your wrist. I'm here to alert you to the next pop cultural phenom: a 12th-century philosopher popularly known as the Rambam.

Just a few weeks ago, I attended the "Aloud" reading series at the Los Angeles Central Library to hear a conversation between Julie Salamon and Steven Leder.

Salamon, a culture reporter for *The New York Times,* is the author of the recent *Rambam's Ladder: A Meditation on Generosity and Why It Is Necessary to Give* (Workman), a well-reported and thought-provoking book that explores the charitable impulse in a post-September 11 context—who gives, how they give and why.

Leder, who has a day job as Wilshire Boulevard Temple's senior rabbi, was there in his capacity as author of *More Money Than God* (Bonus Books). Leder's book addresses how money can be a positive force in our lives, providing satisfaction, gratification and enriching our lives beyond the mere accumulation of wealth.

So, on this summer night in 2004, when these two interpreters of secular life were talking about the Rambam, I took this as not as a coincidence but as a trend.

Rabbi Moses Ben Maimon—a.k.a. Maimonides, a.k.a. Rambam—was a physician, philosopher and Jewish community leader. Born in Cordova, Spain, he was forced at age thirteen to flee with his family when the Almohads, a radical Muslim sect, took over.

His family traveled across North Africa. They tried living in what is today Israel, but like many a visitor to the Holy Land, they found it a nice place to visit, but life among the Israelites and Palestinians too difficult to actually reside there. Maimonides and family settled outside of Cairo. The Rambam became a physician to the royal court, had a private practice and lived in Egypt until his death in 1204.

So why are the writings and beliefs of a man who died 800 years ago suddenly in vogue today?

Salamon explained that her editor, Susan Bolotin, had first suggested the Rambam's eight levels of giving as a structure for the book. The highest degree is to give a loan, a job or enter into partnership with someone so that the recipient need not beg; the lowest is to give reluctantly.

"I was constantly amazed by how much of his writing resonated with me," Salamon wrote via e-mail, "enough to draw me through passages that would seem extremely chauvinistic by today's standards."

Leder, for his part, said: "The things he is writing about are precisely the questions that people come into my office about: The veracity of Torah, God and the problem of evil; the balance in religion between the rational and the spriritual; the desire to understand, differentiate and explain differences with the Muslim world."

Maimonides had a brother who was a foreign jewel trader, whom he loved deeply and who traveled to make the money to support the Maimonides family. Each time his brother boarded a ship, Maimonides asked God to grant his brother safe passage. It worked a few times, but then his brother perished at sea.

Leder believes this is a key event in the Rambam's life. The Rambam could have renounced prayer and God; he could have cursed riches and the pursuit of money. Instead, he sought to explain how reason and belief could co-exist.

David Ellenson, the president of Hebrew Union College-Jewish Institute of Religion, feels that Maimonides' appeal is that he spoke of "the universal and the particular." He took all of Jewish law, Ellenson explained, and wrote a "second Torah" the Mishneh Torah, writing in Hebrew so that Jews throughout the world would be able to read a clear and organized iteration of Jewish laws. He then wrote a very difficult disquisition, *The Guide for the Perplexed,* a scholarly philosophical text meant for the intellectual elite but written in accessible Arabic. Ellenson feels that the Rambam's ideas continue to resonate, because "they strike us as correct." Maimonides expressed the best in Jewish thought, he says, and that appeals to all Jews from Reform to Orthodox.

But Maimonides was interested in communicating the truths of Jewish thought not just to Jews but to all people. Just as he treated both Jews and non-Jews as a physician, he wrote in Hebrew and Arabic so his work could be understood by all people.

At a time when the religious decried "Hellenization" (assimilation), the Rambam applied Aristotlean logic to explaining Jewish law. His Judaism existed in a secular world, his faith was an eternal truth.

In addition to classifying eight rungs of charitable giving, Maimonides distilled Jewish thought to thirteen principles. "He redacted without reducing," Leder said. "He made it simple without simplifying."

This is a good thing. I tried reading *The Guide to the Perplexed* and it is tough going. But reading the condensed version is fine. Kenneth Seeskin's "Maimonides: A Guide for Today's Perplexed" (Behrman House) is helpful. But fear not, we are at the start of a Rambam wave, and one need but stay afloat to ride along.

Next year, Sherwin Nuland, a surgeon and author of the critically acclaimed *How We Die,* will publish his own book on Maimonides (Nextbooks/Schocken). Nuland believes that the Rambam is an example of a unique personality who appears among us every so often as an inspiration, as "a rallying force." "If such people can exist, there is hope for all mankind," Nuland said.

Every so often, a writer and philosopher speaks to us across the chasm of time. The Rambam's time is now. You heard it here first: Welcome to the Maimonides fest, or as I like to call it, the Rambamalama.

July 30, 2004

Tough Guys

Isaac Babel

Reading *The Collected Stories of Isaac Babel* (W. Norton & Co., 2002) in paperback, edited by Babel's daughter, Nathalie, got me thinking about Jewish gangsters and tough guys.

Babel was born in Odessa in 1894. He wrote of Odessa's Jewish underworld and its gangsters in sparkling prose. Fifty years before Mario Puzo gave us *The Godfather,* Babel offered up Benya Krik. Benya, Babel tells us, had "gangster chic"—a century before Tupac took the stage. Babel's Odessa was home to a universe of Jewish murderers, pimps and crooks. Before there was 50 Cent, Babel wrote of a millionaire named "Yid and a half."

Although Babel displayed great affection for his characters, he did not seek to glorify their actions. The appeal of Babel's stories is that he stands in the footsteps of the reader, an outsider who is alternately awed, impressed and horrified by these colorful characters and their world.

He accomplished a similar feat in his *Red Cavalry* stories. As a war correspondent for the Bolsheviks, Babel rode with the

Cossacks and wrote journalistic dispatches from the battlefield that have a combination of immediacy and literary fluency that I can only compare to Stephen Crane—and I would say that, of the two, Babel is the greater stylist.

Babel's ability to put himself in a situation alien to his intellectual temperament is what makes the stories hold up to this day (the excellent new translation by Peter Constantine helps, as well, giving the stories more immediacy than the prior versions). As a reader, Babel was known to enjoy reading Sholem Aleichem; as a writer he left the shtetl and the stereotypes behind.

The problem is that Babel launched a romanticization of the Jewish gangster, the "Tough Jew," a love affair that afflicts Jewish self-image to this day.

Let's face it: Jewish gangsters are not in short supply. Last year, Los Angeles witnessed the arrest of several Israelis who were running one of the country's largest ecstasy drug rings. I myself spent a certain amount of time with a former Brighton Beach Russian mobster. He was Jewish, as were most of the gangsters of his wave of immigration. They were the beneficiaries of the Student Struggle for Soviet Jewry, and, since his career of intimidation, extortion, robbery and murder began in the USSR, I'm sure they weren't too sad to see him leave. Here in the United States, he participated in jewelry robberies, scams, tax frauds, extortion and several murders. I had dinner at his home with his wife and child. Nice guy. Haimish. Unless you crossed him.

One of my favorite books about Jewish gangsters is Robert Rockaway's *But He Was Good to His Mother* (Gefen, 2000), a book that tells the story of such murderers and criminals as Abner "Longy" Zwilman, Meyer Lansky and Bugsy Siegel. Rockaway makes clear that, in the end, crime did not pay.

One can argue that where Jews were denied equal access to financial success, they turned to crime. Certainly demographically, it is clear that the age of the American Jewish gangster is on the wane and that today the Russian mob is no longer dominated by Jews. As Jews have ascended to the ranks of professionals, American Jewish criminals have become increasingly white-collar.

Notwithstanding the reality of Jewish gangsters, past and present, there is a danger to glorifying or sentimentalizing their actions—of mythologizing the Jewish gangster into a cult of tough Jews. This notion reached its apex in a wrong-headed book called, not surprisingly, *Tough Jews: Fathers, Sons and Gangster Dreams* by Rich Cohen (Vintage Books, 1999), otherwise an excellent journalist and writer. This may be going out on a limb, but I find it misguided to argue that when Jews are considered wimps or nerds, a vicious gangster is a positive role model.

Don't get me wrong: There have always been tough Jews, going back to Samson, and including the famous Circus strongman Breitbart, boxers Max Baer and Bummy Davis and wrestler Goldstein. But, similarly, there have also always been less-than-tough Jews who bested their tougher opponents. Not to state the obvious but if David were a he-man, defeating Goliath would have been no big deal.

In this regard it is important to note the difference between gangsters, tough guys and heroes. The Maccabees, the Taliban of second century B.C.E. Jerusalem, were tough guys and may have been heroic in their last stand, but they were not always good guys.

A sociopath like Bugsy Siegel, despite Warren Beatty's gloss on him, was certainly a tough guy and a gangster, but he was no hero. By contrast, Moses would probably qualify as criminal—to the Egyptians—tough guy and hero.

Some of this is, of course, situational. A Jew who commits forgery, lies and steals during the Holocaust as a matter of survival may well be a hero. But after the war, if he does it again, he's a criminal.

Idealizing tough guys can get us into all sorts of trouble. Israel's early propaganda was all about creating the new Jew. The heroic Jew. Moshe Dayan with his eye patch was an iconic tough guy and the Six-Day War a heroic battle. But since then, one Lebanon and two intifadas have made a whole generation hostage to a tough situation, where living an ordinary life is heroic, and those military figures, who in other times might be heroes, are now politicians searching for an end to violence that has no heroic end in sight. At least for me, the romance is gone. In our heart of hearts, can we console ourselves by saying: "We'll always have Entebbe"?

Which brings me back to Babel. His stories stand the test of time because they spoke a truth about human desires and behavior, and because he found a fresh way to write about people who had never before been the subject of literature. But once the Russian revolution soured and asked of Babel not truth but "socialist realism," he found it increasingly difficult to write or publish. On May 15, 1939, he was arrested by the secret police. All his papers were confiscated. On January 26, 1940, there was a twenty-minute trial at which Babel was found to be a spy. He was executed that same year. The Soviet Union exonerated him in 1954, but his manuscripts were never recovered.

Isaac Babel was one tough Jew.

August 13, 2004

Einstein in California

One hundred years ago, Einstein was a Zurich Polytechnic teaching graduate who couldn't land a job in academe. Instead, he got a position as a patent clerk in Bern, Switzerland. Not the most challenging job, but it gave him time to think.

Einstein liked to conduct what he called "thought experiments," one of which asked: "What would a beam of light look like if you could race besides it?"

During the course of 1905, what has come to be called Einstein's "miracle year," he published four scientific papers, including his paper on "special relativity," which answered the question posed above. The answer is easier understood today if you replace the beam of light with a car. From the sidewalk, the car looks like it's speeding by. But if you drive alongside the car, it doesn't seem to be moving. By demonstrating the relativity of time and space, Einstein unshackled the perception that they were absolutes.

Within a decade, Joyce wrote *Ulysses,* a chronicle of a single day rendered in stream of consciousness; Proust was working on his own meditation on space and time, R*emembrance of Things Past*; Picasso painted *Les Demoiselles D'Avignon* and made his first abstract sculptures; Nijinsky danced to Stravinsky's *Rites of Spring*; while in Vienna, Freud was conducting his own thought experiments, charting a psychic interior world as unexplored as space itself.

A coincidence? Or a reaction to the industrialization of society? Either way, the reaction to the zeitgeist of relativity in science and culture was quickly followed by World War I and the Russian Revolution. Einstein began his search for a unifying principle of physics, perhaps in order to envision a universe where opposites would co-exist rather than clash.

Einstein made three visits to California in the early 1930s, working at Caltech in Pasadena. As described in *A Lone Traveler: Einstein in California* by Rabbi William Kramer with Margaret Leslie Davis, which the Skirball is publishing in connection with its "Einstein" exhibit, Einstein received the star treatment: Studio owner Carl Laemmle led Einstein on the Universal tour and invited him to a screening of the anti-war classic *All Quiet on the Western Front.* Jack Warner (one of the original Warner brothers) told him, "You know, I have a theory about relatives, too—don't hire them."

Einstein met all Hollywood's then-reigning stars as well as Los Angeles' Jewish elite. He dined at Pickfair with America's sweetheart Mary Pickford and her husband Douglas Fairbanks. He ate on several occasions at Charlie Chaplin's and was his guest at the premiere of *City Lights,* where Einstein's fame seemed to eclipse Chaplin's. He attended services and played violin at Temple B'nai Israel in Pasadena. He conferred with Wilshire Boulevard Temple's Rabbi Edgar Magnin. He spoke at Jewish fundraisers supporting a Zionist homeland and the creation of Hebrew University in Jerusalem.

It would be easy to argue that these visits were insignificant, but in fact California was a turning point in Einstein's life—in many ways it shaped the second part of his life.

The Skirball is offering a special interactive exhibit on Einstein in California, "Three Winters in the Sun," created by USC/ Annenberg's Labyrinth Project. Not part of the New York Museum of Natural History show, the installation focuses on six compartments of Einstein's world: his own household, science, émigrés, Jews, Hollywood and the FBI, which began a file on Einstein that eventually reached 1,400 pages.

Labyrinth Project Director Marsha Kinder, a professor of critical studies at USC, believes Einstein's time in California was "transformative."

For example, consider Einstein's friendship with Chaplin. Einstein found in Chaplin and his "Little Tramp" a simpatico spirit. Erik Erikson and Roman Jakobson have written about Einstein's use of nonverbal language: Einstein's great salve was music; his most eloquent expression was in mathematics. Chaplin was also a master of nonverbal communication. Even after sound was introduced, Chaplin's tramp remained silent.

Einstein learned of fame from Chaplin. When Einstein asked Chaplin under the glare of klieg lights what it all meant, Chaplin replied, "Nothing, absolutely nothing." But Einstein knew better. He used his celebrity to speak out for pacifism, for Zionism and against the Nazis.

Perhaps Einstein had some impact on Chaplin as well: When Chaplin bade farewell to the tramp, his first sound comedy was the anti-Hitler, anti-fascist satire *The Great Dictator.*

By the end of Einstein's third sojourn in California, Germany had come under the force of its own unifying theory: National Socialism. Einstein realized that he would have to give up his home and live as an émigré in America. Einstein also accepted that his celebrity imposed a responsibility and a duty to speak out. As Kinder pointed out in a recent conversation, as the most famous living Jew at the time, Einstein was living denial of Hitler's claims of inferiority.

Anti-Semitism made Einstein a Jew and an even more ardent Zionist. Einstein's God, like his science, was a unifier, not a divider—and if his mathematical formulas tried to explain how planets and atoms should behave, his religion attempted to do the same for people.

As Einstein said at a 1931 Jewish National Fund dinner held at the Ambassador Hotel in Los Angeles: "Out of our community of interests there has at all times risen men who have embodied the conscience of the western world, men who were defenders of humanity and justice."

George Dyson, the science historian, wondered in the Einstein issue of Discover magazine, "What if Einstein had stayed at Caltech?" Expounding on his "What if?" Dyson told me "We will never know....but what if he surfed?" Would Einstein, living in California, among the stars in heaven and on earth, have figured out the ultimate fate of the universe?

We have crossed from the twentieth to the twenty-first century on a wave of technological and scientific innovation. Yet, as we become increasingly interconnected in a rush of globalization, our current modernity has provoked another outbreak of war, extremism and anti-Semitism.

Einstein is back in California, at the Skirball until May 2005. More than ever, Dr. Einstein, we need a theory that will reconcile that which polarizes us.

September 3, 2004

See Jane Shlep

Yiddish with Dick and Jane

"See Jane shlep,
Shlep, Jane shlep,
Shlep, shlep, shlep."

This is not your parent's primer. This is *Yiddish With Dick and Jane,* a new parody by Ellis Weiner and Barbara Davilman, who will be reading their work this Sunday, September 19 at the Skirball Cultural Center.

The story of how Dick and Jane came to be flavoring their speech with Yiddish began innocently enough two summers ago, when Weiner and Davilman found themselves in Laguna with three hours to kill before a performance at the Laguna Playhouse.

"What do we do now?" Weiner asked.

"We can schmy around," Davilman responded. (Schmy: knock about, meander.)

"Or maybe" Weiner said, gleefully, "we can use my favorite word of yours."

"Spatier?" (Spatier: to stroll casually, to take a constitutional.) Yes, We can spatier."

They marveled at how Weiner's family, who came from Russia, the Pale, or even perhaps beyond the Pale, used "schmy," while Davilman, who's roots owed more to the Austro-Hungarian Empire, used "spatier."

Soon they were kidding each other.

Davilman said, "See Jane spatier," and Weiner said, "This is a book."

The more they thought about it, the more they agreed.

Weiner's credits as a humorist are longstanding and extensive. As his bio indicates, Weiner has been an editor of the National Lampoon, a columnist for Spy and his work has appeared in *The New Yorker.*

Yiddish With Dick and Jane completes a hat trick of sorts for Weiner, who this year also published a mystery novel, *Drop Dead My Lovely* (New American Library), and *The Joy of Worry* (Chronicle), with illustrations by Roz Chast. As far as humor goes, you might call him a maven.

Davilman has written for advertising agencies, started her own greeting card company and has written for TV and film. This is their first book together.

"Mazel Tov" one might say—but that is as much Hebrew as Yiddish.

Still, *Yiddish With Dick and Jane* was not an easy sale. Weiner and Davilman wrote the text in full and then submitted it to 14 editors, all of whom passed. Either they didn't get it or loved the idea, but the legal departments said, "Are you meshugge?"

Actually what they said was, "No way."

Finally, the book was submitted to Little Brown, a division of Time Warner, and they loved it. They just asked that Weiner and Davilman find the illustrator themselves.

This led to an Internet search that auditioned illustrators from all over the world before finding Gaby Payn, who lived next door to Davilman, literally. Her fifties retro-style watercolors play a nice counterpoint to the text, as comforting as the text is subversive. Payn was a hilf. (Hilf: a godsend.)

What Weiner and Davilman succeed at so brilliantly is bringing Dick and Jane into a present in which Jane sells real estate, Dick schmoozes on the golf course and grandma has a stroke—causing all to say, "Oy vey!" They also call Jane's sister, Sally, who teaches transgressive feminist ceramics in Berkeley.

Sally, having left the seemingly perfect world that Dick and Jane inhabit, is the character with her eyes open—who knows that seeing Phil and Susan at the Chinese restaurant without their respective spouses means they are shtupping (shtupping: if you don't know this expression, I'm not going to be the one to tell you)—and who points out that Susan's actions are better understood when they see her husband, Tom, kissing Phil.

This combination of nostalgia for how things were, combined with evidence that nothing is as it seems, is a comic concoction both arch and wise.

This is the America of third- and fourth- and fifth-generation Jews, the children of parents who never spoke Yiddish but passed along certain expressions and phrases to leaven life. The children of the country club Jews of "Goodbye Columbus," suburban all-Americans who beg the question: Can you still call it assimilation, when it was your great-grandparents who assimilated?

And what does it say about assimilation when your non-Jewish friends and business associates know and use more Yiddish expressions than you? For my European-born parents, Yiddish was a lower-class language they were striving to never use or hear again. For my daughter, it will probably be a class she takes in college—and that, as Woody Allen said in "Broadway Danny Rose," is the emess (the truth).

Yiddish With Dick and Jane provides a glossary of terms to brush up your Yiddish. The spellings are phonetic rather than authentic. By contrast, the definitions are traditional, rather than colloquial, which is to say that many people, myself included, use Yiddish phrases inaccurately—which you might say is a shanda but you would be technically wrong (i.e., I use shanda to mean "a shame" but is meant more precisely to imply a scandal and an affront to decency).

Still, Weiner and Davilman could not include as many terms as they wanted to in this first effort. So there will hopefully be a bissele more *Yiddish with Dick and Jane.* (Bissele: a little.)

Then Weiner and Davilman hope to take them on the road to Hollywood, to the hood....but first, there is the Skirball this Sunday, and then a trip across the country visiting Jewish Book Fairs in November.

See Weiner and Davilman schmooze.

Schmooze Weiner and Davilman.

Schmooze, schmooze, schmooze.

September, 17 2004

Cleaning House

Several months after my mother died, I had to clean out her apartment in New York. The apartment had sold, the co-op board had approved the new buyers, the closing was imminent. The apartment had to be delivered empty.

This was the apartment I had grown up in, where my parents had lived, where my father had died more than seven years ago.

My parents were from the Old World, and the apartment reflected that. The rooms were dark, filled with chandeliers, heavy furniture, Louis XV-style gilt-edged pieces, rugs upon dark rugs and gloomy Dutch master-style portraits.

The apartment was filled with "stuff'—or crapola, as it might have been called in other times. It's not so much that my mother was a pack rat. My father was more of one—he was attached to papers, speeches he had given, awards he had received—the documentary evidence of his considerable personal and philanthropic accomplishments.

My mother, on the other hand, liked knickknacks (I believe the correct technical term is tchotchkes). Bric-a-brac filled the house, arranged in her idiosyncratic way—one of my favorites was a netsuke of a wizened Japanese man, into whose fists my mother had placed an Israeli flag on a toothpick.

The process took two days: On the first, I went through everything, room by room, picking out those items that I would keep—there were books, one of my dad's awards, a painting that would have been thrown out and that little netsuke. There was a whole basement bin that had to be gone through, and down there among the unused luggage I found a box of my juvenilia—some paperback Hermann Hesse novels in the Noonday edition and items collected on a summer vacation to England at fifteen.

As long as I focused on the task at hand, the time went by. Deciding on what was going to the auction house vs. what to charity, tossing out a bag of shoes that no one would take. People came and went: my father's cousin, his wife, my mom's friend (and her bookkeeper), a woman who worked at a charity thrift house to which we wanted to donate some items.

The new owner's engineer came to look at the radiators. His name was Zoltan and said the apartment reminded him of being back in Budapest.

The second day was moving day: The auction house sent movers to pack everything up. I boxed up those items I was keeping. The papers and photos that I couldn't deal with now but wanted to, at some future date, I boxed as well (they are still in the box). In the end, what I kept amounted to eight boxes, a filled suitcase, a painting. In the end, more than I expected, less than several lifetimes' worth.

One might have thought that an empty apartment would be less oppressive than a filled one. In my imagination, it was a dark apartment. Now as the late afternoon sunlight filled the rooms, it was larger and brighter and seemed to fill up with ghosts.

As I walked through the apartment one last time, time ran in reverse. This was the room my mother died in, this the room my father died in. I recalled parties in the living room, birthday and holiday dinners in the formal dining room, everyday meals in the kitchen. Here I sat in the afternoons and evenings doing my homework.

As I looked at the rooms, I saw them in all their various configurations and decorations over the years. The mirror was there, the bunk bed fit in there—there used to be bookshelves and a window seat there.

I remembered the first night we moved in, more than 40 years ago, in January 1961. We were waiting in the empty, new apartment for the furniture to arrive. It was already late and the movers hadn't shown up. It seemed as if they never would. We sat in the window seat, and my mother put my head in her lap and told me to fall asleep there. What dreams awaited us all!

The memories and the ghosts almost overwhelmed me right there and then, but then a shaft of sunlight lit upon my face, and they were gone. It was just an empty apartment that I was standing in.

Like the apartment, my mother's death left me empty—yet at the same time, I was a shell filled with memories. As I stood at the apartment door, I was the little boy leaving for school, my mother giving me a thumbs-up sign to have a good day. I was the college boy fumbling at the door coming home for vacation. I was a young man bringing his wife, carrying his baby daughter to see her grandmother for the first time. I was a middle-aged man visiting his sick mother, entering the apartment to be at her deathbed.

Now I had to go. The apartment was empty—soon it would belong to someone else. I closed the door for the last time and pressed the button for the elevator. Another life would be built there.

For me, the apartment was now in the past. But the memories I took with me. They would always be present.

October 1, 2004

Listening to Lenny

Lenny Bruce

One night many, many years ago, I was at The Comedy Store on amateur night when Robin Williams walked in off the street and jumped onto the stage. For the next forty-five minutes, the air inside the club turned into nitrous oxide as Williams made us all feel a bit brighter, a bit wittier, a bit more manically high just for being able to keep up with him. It felt like being inside a comic mind that was both unhinged and unleashed.

A few years later, I was lucky enough to see a preview performance in New York of a one-woman act by a performer with the unlikely name of Whoopi Goldberg. Throughout the performance, which later moved to Broadway (and is now scheduled to return for a twentieth anniversary performance), I was often uncertain of whether to laugh at or be scared of the characters she created onstage. Either way, I knew I was in the presence of a performer whose abilities as a social commentator and as a mimic were conjoined in an unforgettable fashion.

I mention this because I've spent the last several weeks listening to the recently released six-CD box set *Lenny Bruce: Let the Buyer Beware* (Shout Factory), an exhaustive and authoritative collection that gives the uninitiated and even the fan a sense of the thrill, the importance and the tragedy of being Lenny Bruce.

The collection offers evidence of Lenny in his prime, riffing like a virtuoso, taking you on an intoxicating journey of language, the combination of hipster slang and Yiddish, mini-dramas told in word pictures. But it also renders Lenny at the end—drug-addled, obsessed, reading legal statutes and his court transcripts and playing tapes of interviews with the jurors from his trials.

The boxed set was a labor of love. Kitty Bruce, Lenny's daughter, knew where all his tapes were kept and wanted them to see the light of day. In 1991, Bob Emmer of Shout Factory asked Hal Willner to produce. Willner, who was known then mostly as a music producer, has since produced an Allen Ginsberg boxed set, as well as live tribute shows to Leonard Cohen and last Spring's Randy Newman evening at UCLA's Royce Hall. Although there would be legal delays, eventually a cut was made. Legendary producer Marvin Worth ("Lenny," "Malcolm X"), who controlled Lenny's estate got involved, making sure Willner balanced rarities with Lenny's greatest and best-known bits. Worth died in 1998 causing further delays, but eventually the parties focused on what was most important: letting Lenny Bruce have the last word.

Lenny's professional trajectory was like that of a shooting star—he came on the scene fast and bright—by 1959 he was no longer just a stand-up; as he put it, "I'm not a comedian, I'm Lenny Bruce." By 1962, however, he was a target—his shows were busted repeatedly for obscenity and Lenny was arrested several times for drugs. By the mid-sixties his trials consumed him and dominated his material. Broke, defeated, he could no longer make a living. He died of an overdose on August 3, 1966.

The boxed set offers live versions of some of his most famous bits, "Moses and Christ," "Religions, Inc.," "The Palladium"; unreleased gems such as Lenny's teenage appearance on *The Arthur Godfrey Show* and a morning performance he did for Jonathan Winters dubbed *The Breakfast Show*; and even a series of unreleased commercials Lenny taped for the Los Angeles clothing store Zeidler and Zeidler.

Movies and TV were Lenny's frame of reference. He started his career doing impressions and throughout his career his ability to mimic stars and figures from current culture enlivened his monologues. His appearances on TV, whether on *The Steve Allen Show* or Hugh Hefner's *Playboy Penthouse,* widened his popularity. Although he tried writing for TV and movies, his true talent was as a performance artist. The best movies he created happened in your imagination as he spoke. He did bits, he told stories, but his free-form monologues were crafted and tempered by the audience on any given night. They were an American art form. They were jazz.

When Lenny's own life became a drama, he couldn't resist talking about the intricacies of his own immolation. He stopped being funny, but he didn't stop being fascinated and fascinating. That is probably why he inspires such loyalty. He was addicted and addictive.

Lenny's fingerprints are all over present culture. Whether in movies that mock recent or current culture such as *Zoolander, Dodgeball, Anchorman,* (basically anything Ben Stiller does) or in the animated fare of *South Park* duo Matt Stone and Trey

Parker. In the world of stand-up, comedy maven Brad Schreiber told me that he hears echoes of Lenny in such comics as Chris Rock and Bill Maher. They are all Lenny's stepsons.

Just imagine what Lenny would have had to say about The Patriot Act or Janet Jackson's "wardrobe malfunction." Hal Willner has said that Mel Gibson's *The Passion of the Christ* made "many of Lenny's bits come to mind and it feels now like Lenny Bruce is needed more than ever."

There is no little irony in the fact that while Lenny's battles with the law broke him, Howard Stern's battles with the FCC have increased his ratings and led to a lucrative Satellite radio deal. Maybe that's progress.

I never saw Lenny Bruce live. But listening to *Lenny Bruce: Let the Buyer Beware* makes me wish I had. After listening to more than seven hours of CDs, it was strange: my head hurt, but I wanted more. The boxed set had given me a taste of something I couldn't have. Man, I wish I could have been in the room then.

October 15, 2004

Visiting History

The cemeteries of LA

I have always had a soft spot for Brazil. I spent the summer after high school graduation there, and my wife and I spent our honeymoon there. I love the people, the music, the food and the spirit that Brazilians carry with them as effortlessly as they dance the samba. But I never imagined my affection for Brazil had a historic basis and a Jewish link.

I mention this because it turns out that the first Jews in America, who arrived 350 years ago, came from Brazil. Those first twenty-three Jews from Recife arrived in New York in 1654, having fled the auto-da-fé that awaited them in their homeland only to be captured by Spanish pirates and rescued by a French vessel eager to ditch them in America. When after their Job-like journey they set foot in this land-o-plenty, Peter Stuyvesant, director general of New Amsterdam, greeted them with a stream of anti-Semitic invective usually reserved for Jews who've resided in a land for at least a few years. Despite his biases they stayed. And flourished.

Over the last centuries, the Jews, as has been remarked by Semite and anti-Semite alike, have succeeded at the highest levels in every industry and profession they have entered including law, medicine, science, manufacturing, the media and the arts. We have seen dreams come true that earlier generations could not even imagine. That the chronicle of Jewish achievement appears to us today self-evident, almost a cliché, doesn't make the last 350 years any less remarkable.

The earliest Jewish residents arrived in Los Angeles in the 1840s, and the impact of American Jews on the city's culture is pervasive. Los Angeles' history and landscape are so rife with the concrete and lasting evidence of Jewish creative accomplishments that the challenge is to find the right prism to celebrate its many cultural heroes. Movies, TV, art museums—take your pick.

So for this celebration of 350 years of Jewish culture in America, I thought I'd invite you to a gathering of some of our most famous coreligionists here in Los Angeles, and take you to some places where you can find, as they used to say at MGM, "More stars than there are in heaven." There is, without fail, but one sure way to see a cavalcade of celebrities in Los Angeles: go to a cemetery.

You want intellectuals, we got those. In Santa Monica, at Woodlawn Cemetery, I've gazed upon the graves of novelists Lion Feuchtwanger and Heinrich Mann, their headstones engaged in eternal conversation.

In Westwood, just one block from Wilshire Boulevard sits the oasis of Pierce Brothers Westwood Memorial Park. There one can commune with director Billy Wilder (who's probably otherwise engaged in a card game with fellow resident Walter Matthau), trade quips with Oscar Levant, recent arrival Rodney Dangerfield or the original "Funny Girl"

Fanny Brice. You might hum a tune to Sammy Cahn or Mel Torme, or pound out a beat to Buddy Rich. If you're mulling over how to close a deal, perhaps some time with Armand Hammer or Swifty Lazar is in order. And if you wish to worship at the altar of beauty, pray pay a visit to Natalie Wood or Marilyn Monroe.

Should you find yourself between pitches to Warner Bros., Universal or Disney, you may want to practice before the luminaries interred at Mount Sinai Memorial Park on Forest Lawn Drive. If it's a comedy, Phil Silvers and Totie Fields are willing to listen; for a disaster movie, consult the master—Irwin Allen; and if it's a TV show you are contemplating the late great Brandon Tartikoff is there to inspire. Need more expert opinions? Forest Lawn next door is the final resting place of Jack Webb, Freddie Prinze and Marty Feldman.

Talk about heroes: This November 11, Mount Sinai will honor Jewish veterans, placing flags on each of their graves as they have every year for the last fifty years. If you know of a Jewish veteran interred at Mount Sinai that they should honor, please call Shelli Spitzer at (323) 769-1371.

The Hollywood Forever Cemetery tucked away behind Paramount Studios, has some of the most gorgeous grounds in all of Los Angeles with a beautiful lake and the mausoleums and memorials of many of Hollywood's earliest pioneers and greatest stars. Studio founders Jesse Lasky and Harry Cohn are there, as well as Paul Muni and Peter Lorre. You can also visit Mel Blanc, the voice behind so many classic cartoons, whose headstone reads, predictably enough, "That's all folks." If you really want to know how to intimidate and influence people, in the southwest corner you will find Beth Olam cemetery, consecrated ground which holds the earthly remains of Benjamin Siegel, better known and feared as "Bugsy."

Finally—and I do mean finally—which one of us has not been driving on the 405 freeway south of Los Angeles, perhaps coming from or going to LAX and not marveled at the giant white stone canopied monument and the water cascading down the green slope at Hillside Memorial Park. Look closely and you can imagine its honoree, legendary entertainer Al Jolson on one knee singing "Swanee."

Hillside is very proud of its roster of stars. As part of this year's national "Celebrate 350" program, Hillside has published *Distinguished Residents,* a who's who of their necropolis, including Jack Benny, Eddie Cantor, Lew Wasserman, Michael Landon, Max Factor, Dinah Shore, Lorne Greene, Hank Greenberg, Allan Sherman, The Three Stooges' Moe Howard and Milton Berle, to name but a few. This book is available for free on a limited basis by calling (800) 576-1994.

As we celebrate 350 years of Jewish life in America, we recall those 23 Brazilian Jews brave enough to travel to this land, resourceful enough to stay. Their inauspicious arrival in this country has been followed by a rich history of Jewish participation in every aspect of American history.

In Los Angeles, America's Jews have found a home where they not only embraced the culture, they created, nurtured and supported it. To marvel and be inspired by the depth and breadth of Jewish cultural achievement is not hard. You need but visit the cemeteries of Los Angeles.

October 15, 2004

Literary Journeys

Memoirs by Jonathan Schwartz, Nessa Rapoport and Stefan Zweig

The most memorable books I've read recently have been, ironically enough, three memoirs that stand out for their sensitivity, intelligence and literary quality.

Jonathan Schwartz's *All in Good Time: A Memoir* (Random House) is a particularly well-crafted, deeply felt story of childhood neglect as the child of famed Broadway and movie music composer Arthur Schwartz, and his own rake's progress surrounded by music as a radio DJ and cabaret performer.

In retrospect, it seems like I spent every night of ninth grade listening to Schwartz's broadcasts on WNEW-FM 102.7. He would play songs by the Beatles and Jimi Hendrix and talk baseball and find connections between things great and small—sometimes illustrated by a rambling story. To me and my friends, Schwartz was our J.D. Salinger and Holden Caulfield (creative genius and misfit) rolled into one. We cared for him, we rooted for him. And then he disappeared. He published some short stories, and a great collection called *The Man Who*

Knew Cary Grant. But when he returned to radio, this time to AM to host a program on Sinatra, he had lost me. With this volume, I hear his voice again. And if this memoir is too short on his FM tenure, the story he tells is both shocking and tender written with a sensitivity usually reserved for fiction.

We get to know a boy so lonely and alienated that he sneaks around Beverly Hills, looking in—and on occasion breaking into—other people's home so he can gather some small flavor of family intimacy. This, as his own mother suffers from a debilitating illness and his father entertains Hollywood's musical elite, such as Bing Crosby, Artie Shaw, Jerome Kern and Judy Garland—who sang lullabies to him.

After moving to New York, Schwartz's mother died and his father remarried the wicked stepmother of every child's fears. Schwartz, not yet a teenager, started to host radio broadcasts from his apartment. He leads us through high school, friendship with the Simon girls, Carly and Lucy, gigs as a radio DJ in Boston, a piano player in Paris and working as a radio DJ in New York. In Paris, man meets obsession when Schwartz is introduced to Frank Sinatra before a performance at L'Olympia.

I've never been much of a Sinatra fan, yet Schwartz makes such a compelling case for the beauty, elegance and artistry of Sinatra's recordings that I had to go out and get a copy of "In the Wee Small Hours." Schwartz offers insights into the mercurial character of the legend that render him a tad more human, if not any more likable.

In the subtlest of ways, and with a deft touch that is as honest as it is unsparing, he describes his history as an alcoholic, a journey that began as a ten-year-old taking sips of whiskey and progressed to the teenager who filled soda cans with alcohol, a habit that floated him through many relationships, several marriages and children of his own, until he found himself asking the Betty Ford Center to admit him.

Schwartz's charm is that we read his journey much like we listen to a blues song—we appreciate the aching even as we see the damage caused by the pain.

Speaking of journeys, my dear friend, Nessa Rapoport, was in Southern California last week for a talk at the JCC in Irvine and an appearance at the Jewish Book Festival of the San Gabriel and Pomona Valleys to promote her new book, *House on the River* (Harmony Books), the story of a summer trip on a houseboat with her children, her mother and her aging uncle and aunt.

I first read *House on the River* last spring and it has stayed with me since. It is that rare thing: a slim volume that reads like a narrative but is in fact poetry. It is wise beyond its words, with insights and observations about the things that matter and the extraordinary quality of small moments. Like fireflies in a jar, Rapoport captures the ephemeral moments among family members that far too often slip between our fingers soon after we promise ourselves we'll remember them forever.

Finally, for the last several weeks, I have been reading Stefan Zweig's *The World of Yesterday.* In the first half of the 20th century, Zweig, a Viennese Jew, was Europe's greatest and best-known literary figure. His novels, short stories, critical and literary biographies were best-sellers, translated into more than 30 languages. Born in 1880, he died in 1942 in Brazil, in a double suicide with his wife—his last message concluded: "I salute all my friends! May it be granted to them yet to see the dawn after the long night! I, all too impatient, go on before."

Zweig recounts not his own story so much as the story of his age, what life was like in the nineteenth and early twentieth centuries, as well as the personalities he befriended such as his first newspaper editor, Theodore Herzl, and his friends Rainer Maria Rilke, Auguste Rodin, Luigi Pirandello, James Joyce, Sigmund Freud and Maxim Gorky. Reading "The World of Yesterday" is like having the most intelligent and perceptive tour guide to the people and places of a world that feels close to one's heart but that with time has become increasingly foreign.

If you have been at all engrossed in the events in our country and the world over the last few months, it is fascinating to take the long view by reading Zweig—to see how much things change—and how much they don't.

Each of these three books have taken me on journeys—emotional and intellectual—that I heartily recommend. And while the airlines we travel on may be going bankrupt, these books will certainly make your life richer, as they have mine.

November 12, 2004

Becoming a Nephew

The Yad Vashem online database

Today, I am a nephew. Last weekend, the names of more than 3 million persons murdered in the Holocaust were posted on the Internet as part of a searchable database created by Yad Vashem in Jerusalem.

Yad Vashem was established in 1950 by an act of the Knesset, the Israeli parliament, as the Holocaust Martyrs' and Heroes' Remembrance authority. From its very inception, it has taken on the task of being a repository for the names and memory of the 6 million Jews murdered by the Nazis and their collaborators.

In the 1950s, researchers at Yad Vashem created a simple form called the "Page of Testimony" to list the names, birthplace, birthdate, place and date of death (if known) of the murdered. In the 1950s, researchers went door-to-door in Israel to gather data. At the same time, visitors to Yad Vashem were encouraged to add their own information.

But even filling out such forms could be difficult. I remember attempting to help my father fill out such a form. As he never talked about his murdered brothers and sisters, he found it difficult to even write their names.

His parents he could name, but not knowing the exact place of their death stymied him. To this day, I'm not exactly sure what information he submitted. But now I should be able to check.

By the mid-1990s, Yad Vashem had gathered 2 million names. As computerization made the possibility of organizing a giant database ever more of a reality, a new push was undertaken to gather names.

My cousin, Mike Sherwood, called me to say he had filled out forms about his family in Tarnopol and encouraged me to submit information I had uncovered during a trip to Ukraine in 1995. I did so (and forgot about it until today).

In 1999, the Swiss bank scandal gave an unexpected boost to the project. The Volker Commission, established to track victims' assets in Swiss Banks, ended up unleashing a chain reaction of people submitting forms to Yad Vashem. One Yad Vashem official estimated that they received an additional 400,000 names as a result.

According to a story this week in The Times of London, over the last five years, more than 1,000 persons worked, sometimes around the clock, to transfer the now more than 3 million handwritten forms to the computer database.

It is, of course, a race against time, as the survivors die out. However, it is expected that their families and relatives will now have a chance to check the databases and this will provide one more wave of submissions.

Nessa Rapoport, who first told me about the database going online, e-mailed to tell me that she was up all night, finding details about relatives that were thought lost to history – these are profound and powerful moments, and I can't wait to read what Nessa writes about her experience. Yad Vashem's Web site (www.yadvashem.org) will launch a thousand (if not millions) of journeys of discovery.

I went online this morning, and although I spent an hour, I have barely scratched the surface. There were six pages on "Teichholz" (the original spelling). There was a whole branch in The Netherlands that I never knew about who were deported and died in transit or camps such as Bergen-Belsen. There were Teichholzes from Kielce, from Tarnopol, Lvov and several other cities I've never heard of.

I have already made discoveries in the database. When I visited Lvov in 1995, I had found a record of a Wolf Teichholz. As he was not part of my father's direct family, I had no idea who he was. I learned this morning that he was related to relatives of my cousin Mike in Tarnopol; that he had a wife, Rachel, and a son, Meier, born in 1930 who all died in 1941.

In the database, I found the listings for my father's parents, Izak and Henia, and his brothers and sisters (Josef, Aron and Sara). When I clicked on Izak, I found his birthdate, his marital status and other information. This was tremendously satisfying.

Still, I can't properly convey the shock I felt when I clicked on the link that explained who submitted the information. What the computer listed was simple. It said: "GRANDSON."

Though I knew my maternal grandmother and was very close to her, I had never been able to imagine myself as a grandson to my father's father. I could barely think of him as a grandfather. He was a person divorced from my consciousness, separated by a lost world, a person lost in the Holocaust, lost to me—hardly my murdered grandfather. Until now, when this simple listing made the loss fresh.

Similarly, I had grown up with no uncles and aunts, no cousins and nieces—only a set of people we called "Uncle" and "Aunt" who were distant relatives. Even my cousin, Mike is, in fact, my father's second cousin. It was similarly shocking to see myself listed on a form about my father's brother, Aron, as his nephew.

A nephew was, I had always believed, something allowed only to people with parents born in America. I was strangely and deeply moved by the fact that I had been a nephew all these years and never really known it.

Today I became a grandson. Today I became a nephew. Across time and history, www.yadvashem.org reminds us what a powerful medium the Internet is, and how an attempt at mass murder and genocide can be undone by the collaborative power of memory.

November 26, 2004

Dancing Queen

Liane Weintraub and Dance in LA

Amid myriad reasons for moving to and living in Los Angeles, let me add one: this is a city where one dedicated individual can still have a major cultural impact.

This came to mind recently when I made the acquaintance of Liane Weintraub, a new mother in her mid-thirties. Weintraub lives in Malibu and no one could blame her for enjoying the life she is fortunate enough to lead. Instead, she has taken on a different challenge. In a short time, she has become Los Angeles' major dance benefactor and a leader in making the city, in her words: "The dance center it always could be."

Born and raised in New York and Denmark in an assimilated Jewish home where culture was revered—her father, a German Jew, had fled Berlin in 1939; her mother ran an art gallery in New York—Weintraub came to Los Angeles a little more than a decade ago. She studied journalism at USC and was a broadcast journalist at KADY (UPN). However, delivering the agricultural report for the Central Valley was not quite the career she had hoped for, so she moved out of the bright lights to ponder what she could do and where she could make a difference.

Weintraub had a passion for dance. It had been sparked as a little girl by ballet lessons and by attending *The Nutcracker,* and it continued even after she herself abandoned dancing. Los Angeles, she felt, was missing a dance series commensurate with the city's importance as a cultural center. Weintraub wondered what she could do about it. She contacted the Music Center downtown. Her timing couldn't have been better.

You might think Los Angeles would be a great Petri dish for classical and modern dance—just consider all the attractive, athletic, body-obsessed, eating-disorder-afflicted denizens of this city. Who could ask for a better pool of dancers and balletomanes? Yet California has always seemed to signify other disciplines—gymnastics, figure skating, cheerleading, surfing or playing volleyball.

The story of creating both an audience and the requisite financial support and patrons for Dance at The Music Center is a long and somewhat troubled saga. Over the last 25 years there have been several major attempts to jump-start dance programs.

Between 1979 and 1983, John Clifford of the New York City Ballet (NYCB) came to Los Angeles with a number of dancers and the rights to a certain amount of Balanchine repertoire. The idea was to create an LA Ballet, but the effort didn't take root.

In 1983, The Music Center invited the Joffrey Ballet to become a bicoastal company. This was a very exciting development to which many people became deeply committed, both as patrons and as an audience. However, in 1991, when the Joffrey decamped to Chicago, as Weintraub says, "People had their hearts broken."

The next phase involved what has come to be known as The Dance Gallery Project, a plan to build a dance center anchored by West Coast modern dance legend Bella Lewitzky and her company. The Music Center undertook a major capital campaign that raised several millions, but the project never came together. Some donors felt their money had gone nowhere and became alienated from supporting dance in Los Angeles.

Weintraub discerned a pattern in the failed initiatives: "What they all had in common was an effort to impose a specific aesthetic or company that LA should have been receptive to, but was not."

Instead of trying to grow a company in Los Angeles, Weintraub joined with others in June 2000 to launch the Center Dance Association of the Music Center (CDA) and became its organizing chair. The idea was to build the audience for dance—rather than for a specific dance company—by presenting world-class international, national and local dance companies at the Dorothy Chandler Pavilion and the Ahmanson Theatre.

At the same time, the launch of Disney Hall created dance-programming opportunities at the Music Center and the redevelopment of downtown made traveling to the center less intimidating.

Weintraub started CDA as a membership organization that supports the best possible dancers and dance companies appearing in Los Angeles, by helping to bridge the gap between ticket sales and the cost of staging the performances.

"We can sell out every seat and not make up the cost of the engagement," she said.

Membership in CDA begins at 1,000 dollars and includes preferred seating, and behind-the-scenes events with dancers and luminaries of the dance world.

At the same time, realizing that not every dance fan can be a patron, Weintraub also just launched Friends of Center Dance, a support organization where for a contribution of as little as 100 dollars you receive a newsletter and are invited to membership events and backstage tours and lectures.

CDA also hopes to grow the audience for dance through their outreach program. CDA has partnered with P.S. ARTS (an organization that restores arts education to public schools, for which my wife is a trustee) to create memorable and valuable experiences for children. For example, they brought students to a working rehearsal of the NYCB to learn about ballet. Also when American Ballet Theater (ABT) performed "Le Corsair," the Music Center held a pirate-themed family fun day.

This is the second full season of Dance at the Music Center. This year has already seen the NYCB in their first appearance in Los Angeles in thirty years (and the first ever at the Music Center) as well as *The Lion King* choreographer Garth Fagen. Coming up this spring is the Beijing Modern Dance Company performing to Pink Floyd's *The Wall.* ABT is returning this spring, along with Merce Cunningham, Bill T. Jones and Arnie Zane and the Eifman Ballet of St. Petersburg in a new production of *Anna Karenina.*

Los Angeles is less stratified, less ossified than most major cities. Almost all the cultural institutions here are the results of singular visions, and individuals choosing to give to the city. Traditionally, Jews were shut out of the dominant cultural institutions—from sitting on their boards or running them. Here they created their own.

Imagine trying to have a similar impact on the cultural scene in New York, Boston, Chicago or San Francisco. One would have to kiss-up to and crawl over, push aside and kill a long line of people to get anything accomplished there. California, however, is a can-do kind of place, a state of mind personified by our philosopher of action, the Governator.

Here's to dance in Los Angeles! I would dance a jig to celebrate, but I prefer to watch. And now, thanks to Liane Weintraub, I can.

December 10, 2004

The Award Goes To…

2004's Funniest moments on screen

As the year ends, many of my correspondents (at least one) have been clamoring for the *Tommywood* Awards, a list of those defining moments in the past year—the best, the worst, the memorable. Frankly, my mind has already gone on vacation and the rest of me is soon to follow. So although I don't rule out a "best of" list early in the New Year, I won't trouble you or myself with that this week.

Instead, the following is a list of things that I actually saw in this calendar year that made me laugh. No big deal, but no small matter either. While rebuilding Iraq and peace in the Middle East may be more worthy goals, let's face it—they didn't provide us with a lot of guffaws.

So what was funny in 2004? What moments of Jewish humor, or humor about the Jews, managed to make me fall out of my seat? Remember, the criteria is funny, not polite; inappropriate is fine by me. This is *Tommywood*, not the American Israel Public Affairs Committee or the Jewish Image Awards. There is no schmaltz allowed at this meal.

I laughed out loud at the opening episode of this season's *Everybody Loves Raymond* where Ray's parents tell him they are moving to a retirement community—and Ray and his brother, Robert, must hide their glee. Jon Stewart had his moments, no doubt, on *The Daily Show*; and for reasons I don't understand, I laughed out loud at the final subtitled animal battle scene in Judd Apatow's *Anchorman.*

All funny.

However, as far as I'm concerned the funniest moment on TV last year occurred on *Survivor,* an episode of *Curb Your Enthusiasm,* which first aired March 7, 2004. As a prelude to Larry renewing his marriage vows on the occasion of his tenth wedding anniversary, he hosted a dinner at his home. His rabbi asked if he might bring along a friend of his who is a survivor and a fan of Larry's work. Larry agrees and then thinks to tell his father to invite his friend who is also a survivor.

At the dinner we discover that his father's friend is a concentration camp survivor while the rabbi's friend is Colby Donaldson, from the Outback season of the reality TV show *Survivor.* Need I say more? Very quickly the two start fighting. Here's some of the dialogue:

Colby: So here we are out in a region of Australia with nine of the world's ten most deadly snakes. It was harrowing! You come across a Taipan on the trail, you get bit, you're dead in 30 minutes flat.

Solly: That's a very interesting story. Let me tell you, I was in a concentration camp. You never suffered one minute in your life compared to what I went through.

Colby: I'm saying we spent forty-two days trying to survive, we had no rations, very little snacks.

Solly: Snacks! What are you talking snacks. We didn't eat sometimes a week, a month....

Colby: I couldn't work out when I was over there.

The two continue to argue over who suffered more until:

Colby: Have you ever seen the show?

Solly: Have you seen our show, it was called The Holocaust!

Colby: All I know is I was damn close to that 1 million dollars, all the time everyone was backstabbing me, undermining me, trying to get me kicked off the show.

Solly: You don't know nothing about survivor. I'm a survivor!

Colby: I'm a survivor!

Solly: I'm a survivor!

Suffice to say the genius of this exchange exists on so many levels—it not only skewers popular culture, but also Holocaust survivors themselves who when introduced often do compare notes, with the not-so-subtle subtext of "who suffered more." For me this ascends into a Pantheon of comic moments, right up there with parts of Mel Brooks and Carl Reiner's *2,000 Year Old Man.*

Where do you go from there? As Hunter Thompson might say, "Just when you thought it couldn't get any weirder..." This was also the year our friends at *South Park* created a very special episode called, "The Passion of the Jew," currently available for rent or purchase on DVD. *South Park* creators Matt Stone and Trey Parker have a particular talent for humor bordering on the anti-Semitic balanced by contempt for everyone else.

In this episode which originally aired on March 31, 2004, Kyle goes to see *The Passion of the Christ* and decides that the Jews are to blame for the death of Jesus and starts to organize rallies for the film's hardcore fans. At the same time, Kenny and Stan think the film is awful and travel to Malibu to demand their money back from Mel Gibson. Offensive? Yes, very. Funny? That, too. You will not soon forget the sight of an animated Mel Gibson dancing in his underwear as he flogs himself.

Finally, in the category of nervous laughter—as in not really funny, but it made me so uncomfortable I had to laugh—first prize goes to the scene of a bar full of patrons in Arizona, singing, "Throw the Jew down the well," as instigated and captured on film by English comedian Sacha Baron Cohen, a.k.a. Ali G. in his guise as Borat on HBO's *Da Ali G Show.*

Also, speaking of inappropriate, "The Best of Triumph the Insult Comic Dog," a collection of Robert Smigel's bits on *Late Night With Conan O'Brien* just came out on DVD. Years ago, I recall a book that asked the question: "Is your dog Jewish?" I can't remember the answer, or for that matter speak to the religious observance of Triumph or his handler (as Triumph is a hand puppet that term is particularly apt) but Triumph's persona harks back to the tummelers of the Borscht Belt—only raunchier.

Some years are less funny than others—and this is what it took this year to make me hold my sides and gasp for air from laughing too hard. You might not agree with my choices and conclude that I am a sick, twisted person, but if these don't make you laugh (even secretly where you're not ashamed to do so), then something's wrong with you. And I sincerely hope you fix it in the coming year.

Or better yet, let me know what you thought were the funniest Jewish moments on TV or film this year at tommywood@jewishjournal.com. You never know, I may just be able to get a column out of your suggestions.

Until then, dear readers, I wish you the best and invite you to laugh with me.

December 24, 2004

Whose Culture Is It?

Does it bother you when a white man sings the blues? Is jazz exclusively an African American art form?

When Eminem (who is white) is the most popular rapper, Tiger Woods (who is part African-American and part Asian) is the greatest golfer and Serena and Venus Williams (African-Americans) dominate women's tennis, should it upset us that Jewish Culture Festivals are run by non-Jews for audiences of primarily non-Jews, and that klezmer music is performed by non-Jewish performers for non-Jewish audiences?

These thoughts came to mind reading Ruth Ellen Gruber's *Virtually Jewish* (University of California, 2002), an account of the renaissance of Jewish culture in Europe often in places where Jews no longer live, and a discussion of the complexities and contradictions it has engendered.

The Philadelphia-born Gruber, who lives in Hungary and Italy, was recently in Los Angeles, visiting family and conducting research for her next book, and I had a chance to hear her give a talk at an event sponsored by the National Foundation for Jewish Culture. A few days later, we met to talk about the explosion of Jewish culture in Europe.

The Jewish Culture Festival in Krakow, Poland, in the Kazmierz district, the former Jewish neighborhood many know from the film, *Schindler's List,* has become—in Gruber's words —"a giant party." Organized in 1988 by two non-Jews, it has become a major arts festival that attracts fans from all over Europe, many (if not most) of whom are not Jewish, for several days of performances lasting late into the night.

Today, there are annual Jewish festivals in Berlin, Munich, Vienna and Budapest. Ancona, in Italy, hosts a festival of Jewish music. This year there was a Yiddish festival in Italy to celebrate the 100th anniversary of the birth of Isaac Bashevis Singer, who has become the portal to the Yiddish world for Jew and non-Jew alike. Above and beyond all this, there has been a boom in Jewish "roots" tourism promoted by the governments of France, Austria, Germany, Poland and Hungary.

Hold on, you may say, how does a European passion for Jewish culture jibe with growing European anti-Semitism? As Gruber explains, they co-exist. It is almost "schizophrenic," she said. For some non-Jews, participating in Jewish cultural events fills the void created by the murder of Jewish communities during the Holocaust. For others, celebrating Jewish culture is a "healing" or it may be a way to expiate guilt; to interact with nostalgic "virtual" Jews, rather than real ones. Not unlike the way Americans have romanticized Native Americans and the Old West (Gruber's next book is about how Europeans have taken up Native American and cowboy culture).

Two decades ago, before the fall of the communism, Jewish historical and religious sites were neglected, in disuse and disrepair. Poland was seen as the "graveyard of European Jewry." It was not a fun trip. Tourists hurried to Auschwitz and other death camps and once sufficiently horrified and chastened, they left the country. Even as late as 1990, it was difficult to find the either reputable guides or the location of sites of Jewish interest in Eastern Europe—or in France, Italy or Spain, for that matter. However, during the mid-1990s all that changed.

Suddenly, there was an explosion of Jewish heritage travel, of the restoration of Jewish sites of interest, of the creation of Jewish museums and Holocaust memorials. Some of the money came from abroad from individuals, institutions and charitable organizations such as the Ronald Lauder Foundation (which was particularly active in Austria, Hungary and Poland). But much more came from the governments themselves—and the creation and management of these new institutions was often carried out by non-Jews. Was this an act of healing or of capitalism? Was it motivated by guilt or greed?

In 1990, the World Monument Fund created a Jewish Heritage Council to identify sites in Europe worth preserving. By the end of the decade, a conference in Paris would celebrate the preservation of several hundred Jewish sites and lay out an ambitious proposal for the reclamation and renovation of hundreds more. Similarly, a 1999 Conference on Jewish Culture for the 21st century held in Paris seeded the creation of a European day of Jewish culture, which is now held annually in cities all across the continent during the first week of September.

Present at many of these conferences was Gruber, the daughter of artist Shirley Moskowitz and Jacob Gruber, an anthropologist, archaeologist and founder of the anthropology department at Temple University.

After graduating from Oberlin College, Gruber traveled to Europe where, as a reporter for UPI, she covered six different countries and spent a lot of time in Vienna, Belgrade and Warsaw. Although not particularly observant (she grew up in a Conservative household) Gruber became part of the "Flying University," a loosely knit group that distributed Jewish books and knowledge to communist Europe.

In January 1983, while covering the Polish Solidarity movement, Gruber was accused of espionage and jailed. She was held for 24 hours and ignited an international protest before she was released and expelled from the country.

During the 1990s, as she traveled in Eastern Europe, Gruber realized that there was no guide to sites of Jewish heritage, so she wrote *Jewish Heritage Travel* (Wiley, 1992), which became a touchstone for many travelers on "roots trips." (Personally, it proved invaluable on my trips to Warsaw, Lodz and Lviv. A great book, it is sorely in need of an update—and a publisher willing to commission one.)

Now she has chronicled what she calls "the mainstreaming of Jewish culture. Twenty years ago, hearing klezmer music and celebrating Jewish culture in Europe was not 'normal'—and the notion of non-Jews celebrating and performing Jewish music and Yiddish literature seemed alarming. Now it is accepted; it is a regular happening."

Yet for Americans, Jewish culture still remains in the shtetl.

Let me give one example: I have a group of friends with whom I travel on an annual basis to New Orleans' Jazzfest. I recently received an e-mail from Ed Serotta who runs www.centropa.org, a Web site devoted to Jewish Central-European history and culture. The e-mail outlined a trip to visit Prague, the Krakow Festival of Jewish Culture and several restored sites of Jewish interest, along with talks by experts (including one by Gruber). In other words, it would be an "all-eating, all-seeing, all-dancing" tour. I passed on the info to my Jazzfest friends.

Their reaction was unanimous, and could easily have been predicted by Reb Jackie Mason: "Too Jewish."

Keep in mind that we are talking about a festival organized by non-Jews, attended mostly by non-Jews that visits sites restored and maintained by non-Jews. Which brings me back to the question: Whose culture is it, anyway?

Perhaps we need to consider Jewish culture, like the five books of Moses, as our gift to the world. An evergreen garden that can nourish Jew and non-Jew alike. And then we should heed the famous coda of Voltaire (a notorious anti-Semite) from Candide: "Cela est bien dit, mais il faut cultiver notre jardin (that may be well said, but we must cultivate our garden)."

January 20, 2005

Was Is Back

A few weeks ago, Sweet Pea Atkinson stood on the stage of the Los Angeles House of Blues, dapper in a red double-breasted, collarless suit, wearing a red fedora and red leather shoes. The occasion was the historic reunion of seminal groove band Was (Not Was) after a fourteen-year hiatus. Sweet Pea grabbed the microphone and proceeded to move the time continuum backward and forward for the better part of a rousing two-hour set.

Turns out Was (Not Was) was, is and continues to be a dance band, a Detroit-born dream of funk contrived by two white Jewish kids who met in junior high, Don Was, nee Don Fagenson; and David Was, nee David Weiss, who not only fantasized about being James Brown but went on to pay proper homage. Their encore consisted of a burning rendition of "Cold Sweat" that would have done the Godfather of Soul proud.

Confession time: Here's how I know Don Was. My wife, a.k.a. the reason people put up with me, plays in a monthly all-women's poker game with Don's wife, Gemma Corfield. As a result, I have had the pleasure of hanging out with Don, who, despite his brushes with music legends, is the most down-to-earth, sweet and funny person you could meet. Plus, he was kind enough to alert me to the historic reunion of Was (Not Was).

In case you missed them the first time around, Was (Not Was) had a good run in the 1980s as Ze recording artists, with two notable hits: "Walk the Dinosaur" and "Spy in the House of Love." Their songs veered from funk classics to art-house wit (i.e., turns out "Dinosaur" is a pop song about nuclear destruction -- who knew?).

However, after the release of their fourth album, *Are You Okay?* (1990), the band paused to pursue "other projects," as the press releases are wont to say. Truth to tell, they got busy.

David Was found himself a great deal of studio work and became the music supervisor on numerous films and TV shows, including *The X-Files.* Today, he does all that and even does commentary for NPR.

Don Was, for his part, found himself in demand as a record producer after Ze Records founder Michael Zilkha asked Don to produce an album by Zilkha's then wife, Cristina Monet (they divorced in 1990). Although Monet's album *Sleep It Off* (1984) had modest sales, Don's work was universally praised (the album has been recently re-issued).

In 1989, Don's career was launched into the stratosphere when Bonnie Raitt's "Nick of Time" swept the Grammies. Don became the producer of the moment—a moment that has seemed to go on to this day. Over the next two decades, Don worked with everyone from Jackson Browne and Bob Dylan to Willie Nelson and the Rolling Stones.

So why reunite Was (Not Was)? Time slipped by too fast. Don Was woke to find himself on the other side of 50, in the studio but not on stage and on the road. Something needed to be done.

Over the years, the band's eclectic constellation has included such diverse seasonings as Wayne Kramer of MC5, Harry Bowens of the OJays, Ozzie Osbourne and even a vocal or two by actress Kim Basinger. This current tour's team features saxophonist David McMurray, guitarist Randy Jacobs, keyboardist Tio Banks and drummer Sergio Gonzalez. Don Was is on bass, David Was provides flute and vocals.

At the House of Blues performance, David Was performed some of his classic Firesign Theatre-like rants, such as "Dad, I'm in Jail" and "I Blew Up the United States," which seem more dangerous than ever in our post-September 11 world.

Was (Not Was) also proved themselves loyal to their Motown roots, performing an amazing cover of the Temptations' "Papa Was a Rolling Stone." This was not without some irony, as Don Was is currently working with the Glimmer Twins, Mick Jagger and Keith Richards, on songs for the next Stones album.

Nonetheless, what came through loud and clear was that Was (Not Was) had returned to proclaim the power of the dance groove. That was the platform on which Sweet Pea intended to campaign, heading out on their reunion tour, which was to continue later in the spring and then into summer, fueling talk of yet another album.

In the meantime, Don Was, dreadlocks intact, stood on stage with a grin as big as Detroit. Up on the balcony of the House of Blues his son from his first marriage, Tony, twenty-six, who as a child had given the band its name, now a grown man, a musician and performer in his own right, stood watch over Don's two young sons, Henry, eleven, and Solly, seven. The kids were dancing, as excited to see their dad perform as they were to be rocking out on a Tuesday night and staying up way past their bedtimes. dThe audience, for the most part contemporaries of the band, were also grinning. They, too, like the band, were excited to be up late, past their bedtimes, in a club, rocking to the music.

February 3, 2005

Death of a Moralist

Although Arthur Miller was only thirty-three when *Death of a Salesman* premiered on Broadway, it was a transformative moment in American drama, and Miller's impact on successive generations of writers continues to this day. In *Death of a Salesman* Miller was able to find poetry in the personal that transcended the mundane—while creating drama that mattered.

Rod Serling, then in his twenties, attended the original production and saw the kind of moral drama about average people that he hoped to write for television; that would seep into Serling's *Patterns* and *The Twilight Zone.* Years later, David Mamet, who would bring to the stage the salesmen of "Glengarry Glen Ross," would be quoted as saying of seeing *Death of a Salesman*: "It was our story that we did not know until we heard it."

Aaron Sorkin, who in *A Few Good Men* and on *The West Wing* challenged audiences to ask "what is the greater good?" when contacted for this article, said: "Mike Tyson on his best day can not send a punch to the chest the way an Arthur Miller play does."

What is so powerful about Miller's work is that although he is often characterized as a moralist, his characters are not ideological straw men—they are deeply flawed, conflicted characters who find themselves blindsided by life.

Miller was the author of seventeen plays, including *The Crucible, A View From the Bridge, After the Fall, The Price, The Ride Down to Mount Morgan* and, most recently, *Finishing the Picture,* which premiered at the Goodman Theater in Chicago in 2004; several screenplays, including *The Misfits, Everybody Wins,* and an adaptation of Fanja Fenelon's *Playing for Time,* as well as short stories (the most recent of which appears in the current Atlantic), several books with his wife, Inge Morath, where he supplied the text to accompany her photos and an autobiography, *Timebends: A Life* (Grove, 1989).

The most recent revival of *Death of a Salesman* with Brian Dennehy is scheduled to open in London on May 16. Miller was working closely on the production until a few weeks before his death.

Miller was the American playwright of the twentieth century and, in some ways, one could argue that the twentieth century was a series of terrible events that no one believed could happen. For Miller, this occurred not just on a historical level but on a personal one as well.

Arthur Miller was born in New York City on October 17, 1915. His father, Isidore, had come to New York as a seven-year-old from Austro-Hungarian Poland and rose from the sweatshop to a successful coat manufacturer whose family lived overlooking Central Park and had a car and driver.

Then the Depression hit, and the Millers moved in with relatives in Brooklyn. Miller could not afford to go to college, but determined to do so, he found work in an automobile parts warehouse, as a lab assistant feeding mice for medical experiments and in the Brooklyn Navy Yard.

Miller attended the University of Michigan, where he won several playwriting contests, but upon returning to New York, he wrote five unproduced plays in a row; the sixth, *The Man Who Had All the Luck,* closed after four performances. By now married, with two children, he decided to try one more time before leaving the theater. *All My Sons,* about a war swindle involving substandard parts that causes the death of twenty-one Army pilots, received rave reviews, two Tony Awards and launched Miller's career.

In 1949, Lee J. Cobb took to the stage in *Death of a Salesman.* By the performance's end the play was acclaimed as an American masterpiece, eventually winning, for the first time, all three top drama prizes—the Pulitzer, the Tony and the Drama Critic's Circle Award—and adding phrases like, "You can't eat the orange and throw away the peel" and Willy's wife's plea that "attention must be paid" to the American lexicon.

However, in many ways, the great dramas of Miller's life were yet to occur. In 1951 at a Hollywood party, director Elia Kazan asked Miller to entertain his girlfriend, Marilyn Monroe. As Kazan watched them dance, he recalled in his autobiography, he saw the future: "How happy she looked in his arms!"

Kazan was summoned before the House Un-American Activities Committee (HUAC). He chose to name names, which angered Miller.

Kazan took *The Crucible* as a personal attack, and Miller chose another director for the play. It received mixed reviews, and Miller restaged it himself six months later.

At the same time, Miller himself was called before the HUAC. Miller would refuse to name names and be cited for contempt of Congress, a charge that the Supreme Court would dismiss in 1958. At the same time, Miller decided to leave his wife and marry Monroe, who herself had divorced American sports hero Joe DiMaggio.

There's an old joke in Hollywood, meant to reveal the low status of writers in Hollywood, about the actress so dumb that she married the writer on her movie. Arthur Miller tried on several occasions to write about the writer so dumb he married the actress. We only have Miller's intimations in his plays "After the Fall" and "Finishing the Picture," his autobiography and those few interviews where he discussed Marilyn, of how blindsided he was by marrying her.

It was a revelation that would appear over and over again in Miller's work. As the actor Stephen Lang put it: "You think you can control life, and you can't."

Five years later, Monroe and Miller would divorce. During that time, Miller wrote not a single play. And although after his divorce from Monroe he married photographer Morath, and he resumed writing plays and continued to do so until his death, Miller never again received quite the acclaim that he did for *Death of a Salesman.*

Throughout the 1960s, Miller spoke out against the Vietnam War and for imprisoned writers as president of International PEN, the worldwide association of writers. Increasingly, however, his plays were not reviewed favorably. Although Miller occasionally groused that in the eyes of critics, early successes only bred later failure, and he resented that his work seemed better appreciated outside the United States than at home, Miller was fortunate to live long enough to have his work re-appraised and his importance as a writer acknowledged by new audiences.

In recent years there have been revivals of *All My Sons;* a film version of Miller's early novel about anti-Semitism, *Focus*; a planned film production of *The Ride Down to Mount Morgan*; as well as the ongoing revival of *Death of Salesman.*

The Crucible, which was made into a 1996 film starring Daniel Day-Lewis (who married Miller's daughter, Rebecca), remains one of the most produced plays in America. There is hardly a high school student in America during the last fifty years who has not seen, read or been in a production of *The Crucible.*

Lang, who appeared in the 1984 revival of *Death of a Salesman* with Dustin Hoffman and in the Goodman theater production of *Finishing the Picture,* explained the ongoing appeal of Miller's works: "Miller is a grownup playwright writing parts for grownup actors."

As a young man, Miller believed that playwriting "was the most important thing a human being could do." Miller's work is often viewed as a product of the Great Depression. But he did not see himself that way.

Others have characterized the moral nature of his work as an outgrowth of the Group Theater in the 1930s and their quasi-Marxist ideals. But in a new introduction to his autobiography, Miller rejected this. Instead, and I believe Miller was somewhat blindsided by this himself, he brought up his Jewishness.

Miller, as he himself admits, is not someone who has spent much time thinking about God or believing that God thinks about him, nor was Miller someone who had much connection with Judaism as practiced in synagogues of any denomination. Here's how Miller put it: "...My resistance to despair seems to have something Jewish about it; some vagrant cell floating through my blood seems to demand that however remote and unlikely ever to be found, a ray of light has to remain after darkness has closed in, a glow of redemption must appear up there at the rim of the pit or the tale is something less than true." And let's not forget that Monroe converted to Judaism to marry him (although his prior and subsequent wives did not).

Miller's plays remain vital and important, because the underlying current in his work demands it. Let this be his epitaph: "Attention must be paid."

February 17, 2005

Kishon: The Funniest Man in the World

The world lost one of its great comic artists last month. I am referring not to Johnny Carson, who was little known outside of the United States, but to Israeli satirist Ephraim Kishon, eighty, who, although little known in America, was beloved around the world. I read somewhere that his books have sold more than forty-three million copies and have been translated into thirty-seven languages (although I can't confirm that there are, in fact, theirty-seven languages to publish in).

Kishon was Israel's most prolific author. He wrote more than fifty books, plays and novels. You can sample his work in a recent collection of greatest hits titled "The Funniest Man on Earth" (Shapolsky). Kishon, a true king of all media, also wrote and directed several movies, including *Sallah Shabati* (1964), which launched Topol's career, *The Policeman* (1970) and *The Big Dig* (1970). Kishon also achieved Hollywood cred: His films have won three Golden Globes and were twice nominated for an Oscar.

I first learned of Kishon from that inestimable connoisseur of comedy, my mother. She gave me a copy of *Look Back, Mrs. Lot!* (Penguin, 1970). One day, when it no longer makes me laugh, I intend to return it. She compared him to Art Buchwald, which dates the reference. Suffice to say, Kishon was Dave Barry, Seinfeld and Jon Stewart all rolled into one (after all, Israel is a small country).

Kishon wrote of the Israeli everyman: plumbers, newlyweds, young parents dealing with their child's pacifier, new waves of immigrants being mistreated by immigrants who had only arrived a short while before, older parents dealing with their grown-up children. Kishon's stories were wry, wise and always revealing of Israeli culture. They were in marked counterpoint to official government propaganda, which portrayed the new Israeli as a Superman.

Today so much attention is focused in the media and on campus on Israel's day-to-day struggles that most students (not to mention most people) know little of the actual internal political structure, literature and culture of the State of Israel. As a response, UCLA is among the first universities in the country to establish an Israel studies program (for more information visit international.ucla.edu/israel/).

Israel's development is such that fifty-seven years after it was founded, you need professors and a whole department to explain Israel's Menshevik-inspired party system and to study the poetry of Mosad Byalik and Yehudah Amichai; the novels of Amos Oz, Aharon Appelfeld and David Grossman; or even the murder mysteries of Batya Gur. Doing so is admirable, and in light of campus anti-Semitic and anti-Israel agitators, necessary and important.

However, for Israel's first thirty years, Kishon's column was the country's own Israel studies department. In Israel's march to becoming a "normal" nation, Kishon chronicled the development of an Israeli consciousness.

I recall one Kishon story that still makes me smile: a guest brings a bottle of wine to a dinner as a gift. When the host discovers he's the victim of regifting (the bottle actually contains chocolates long gone bad), he decides to track down the original giftor, only to discover that he has opened and ruined Israel's only gift and he must now buy a new one for the nation to start the cycle of regifting all over again.

Ephraim Kishon was born Ferenc Hoffman in Budapest in 1924. Son of a middle-class Jewish family, he was barred from university because of the Hungarian anti-Jewish legislation and became a goldsmith. As the Hungarian fascists came to power, he was conscripted into forced labor and was sent to several concentration camps. On one occasion, a Nazi officer lined up prisoners, including Kishon, and shot every tenth man, just skipping him. Another time, the commandant was looking for a chess partner and Kishon survived by playing him, while others were sent to their death. Still later, Kishon was placed on a train transport destined to Sobibor, the Polish extermination camp, and managed to escape.

In life, as in comedy, timing is everything. Or as Kishon later wrote, "They made the mistake of letting one satirist live." He survived the rest of the war by posing as a Slovak laborer named Stanko Andras.

Kishon returned to Budapest at war's end. He wrote for a satirical publication but found the Stalinist regime not to his taste. After arranging a trip to Prague, he managed to escape. In 1949, he immigrated to Israel. According to a Kishon tribute Web site, "The name Ephraim Kishon was given to him by an immigration officer."

At first Kishon lived in a reception camp and then a kibbutz, working at a variety of odd jobs while learning Hebrew. Within two years he had published his first satire, "The Blaumlich Canal," in the newspaper Davar. Shortly thereafter, he started writing a regular column in the newspaper Maariv.

The height of Kishon's popularity came around the time of the Six-Day War. In his columns Kishon captured the atmosphere of Israel under siege, as seen by a Holocaust survivor who was as surprised to be under attack as he was to see his country triumph, which he mined to great effect in such works as *So Sorry We Won* (Ma'ariv, 1967).

Around this time, Kishon's books began to appear in German. He developed a huge following in Germany, which pleased him to no end. He was delighted, his son told newsmen, "That the children of my hangmen are my admirers."

By the 1980s, Kishon found himself once again an outsider, no longer an immigrant, but not a sabra either, alienated from the literary establishment and troubled by what was going on in his country. He started to write opinion pieces.

Writing in the Jerusalem Post, Kishon recalled, "One day, in other words, I realized that I was growing rather more interested in the PLO's doings up in Lebanon than in the plumber's down my drains....maybe it's also a matter of age. A man can't write and write without getting a little older."

Some preferred his humor to his politics, some his politics to his books, still others his movies to his books or his politics.

Kishon began spending part of the year in Switzerland, a country from which he could write about the Israel he was proudest of (without having to put up with too many of what he called the generation of "self-conscious Israelis"). A new country provided Kishon with new comic fodder. In one of Kishon's funniest works, *Land Without Fleas,* he chronicles his attempt to litter in a Zurich held to Swiss standards of cleanliness.

Kishon died of heart attack on January 29, 2005, in Switzerland. He was at work on a new novel. He once said: "I'm not a writer. I'm just a humorist. Only when you are dead, you become a writer."

Ephraim Kishon, Israel's greatest humorist and most prolific author is now one of its greatest writers. The writer, whom to millions was Israel, is now part of its history. Just as Kishon studied Israel, his work remains for future generations to study, and for people everywhere to enjoy.

February 24, 2005

ACKNOWLEDGEMENTS

Journalism is no solitary enterprise. I want to thank all the individuals featured in this volume who were so generous with their time and/or their work and allowed me to tell their stories; as well as their publicists, agents, and/or attorneys, and the artists, curators and communications executives who helped out, granting access and even suggesting stories. I also want to thank Rob Eshman, Susan Freudenheim and all the editors and staff at the *Jewish Journal of Los Angeles* for making my work read better than it should—they share in credit for whatever pleasure you may have in reading my work; any faults remain mine alone. I am grateful to my wife, Amy, and my daughter, Natasha, for their indulgence and support. Finally, I want to acknowledge and my devoted *Tommywood* readers all over the world who, to paraphrase Cameron Crowe's Jerry Maguire, make my writing complete.

About The Author

Tom Teicholz is an award-winning journalist, producer and content consultant who has created print, video and social media content for Intel, The Museum of Tolerance, The Milken Family Foundation, as well as for several not-for-profits and private clients. His work has appeared in *The New York Times Sunday Magazine*, *The Los Angeles Times* Op-Ed page, Newsweek.com, *The Paris Review*, *The New Yorker*'s Talk of the Town, *Narrative Magazine*, and the *Huffington Post*. He lives with his wife and daughter in Santa Monica, CA.

www.ingramcontent.com/pod-product-compliance
Lightning Source LLC
Chambersburg PA
CBHW020608110726
47899CB00002B/422

* 9 7 8 0 9 8 8 3 9 6 4 4 9 *